PENGUIN BOOKS

PASSPORT TO LIBERTY

Jan Sammer was born in Plzen, Czechoslovakia. In 1966 his family escaped from Czechoslovakia and, after six months spent in Austrian refugee camps, settled in Canada in 1967. He attended Sir George Williams University in Montreal (B.A., Major in Economics) and later Columbia University in New York (Master of International Affairs). He is a citizen of Canada and Czechoslovakia and currently resides in Prague.

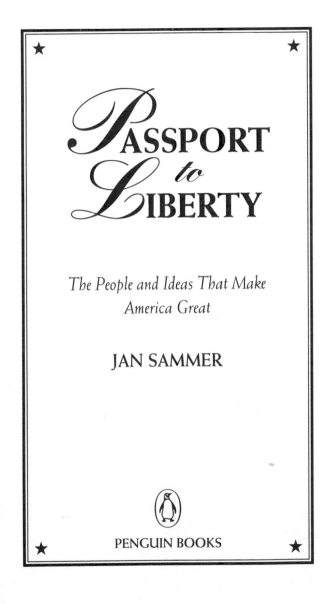

PASSPORT to LIBERTY

The People and Ideas That Make
America Great

JAN SAMMER

PENGUIN BOOKS

PENGUIN BOOKS
Published by the Penguin Group
Viking Penguin, a division of Penguin Books USA Inc.,
375 Hudson Street, New York, New York 10014, U.S.A.
Penguin Books Ltd, 27 Wrights Lane,
London W8 5TZ, England
Penguin Books Australia Ltd, Ringwood,
Victoria, Australia
Penguin Books Canada Ltd, 10 Alcorn Avenue, Suite 300,
Toronto, Ontario, Canada M4V 3B2
Penguin Books (N.Z.) Ltd, 182–190 Wairau Road,
Auckland 10, New Zealand

Penguin Books Ltd, Registered Offices:
Harmondsworth, Middlesex, England

First published in Penguin Books 1992

3   5   7   9   10   8   6   4   2

LIBRARY OF CONGRESS CATALOGING IN PUBLICATION DATA
Passport to liberty: the people and ideas that make America great/
[edited by] Jan Sammer.
p.   cm.
Includes bibliographical references.
ISBN 0 14 01.6967 9
1. United States—History—Sources.   I. Sammer, Jan N.
E173.P27   1992
973—dc20   91–41693

Printed in the United States of America
Set in Weiss

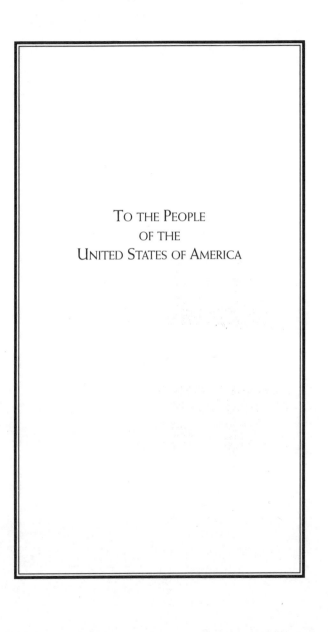

To the People
of the
United States of America

CONTENTS

DOCUMENTS

THE QUEST

THOSE who took part in the American Revolution considered it an event so momentous that it inaugurated a new age in world history. And in truth, at its very conception, the young republic began to exercise an unusual power in its territory and self-confidence abroad, pronouncing itself a champion of liberty the world over. For more than two centuries it has not swerved from this purpose, and what once seemed a quixotic quest has come close to being an accomplished fact.

What is the secret of America's greatness? How did this nation become free and independent in the face of overwhelming odds? How did it remain free, emerging revitalized from crises that on more than one occasion threatened to destroy it? If anyone knows, it is those who made the revolution, as well as those who subsequently tried to live by its ideals and to reinterpret its message for succeeding generations.

In this book we call upon thirty-eight great Americans to be our witnesses. Their statements were made in their own historical context and under specific circumstances, but they are precise, and together they give an unequivocal answer to our quest. We do not believe that this answer needs any further elaboration or interpretation on our part; any such commentary by us would only prejudice the outcome. Hence we have limited ourselves to some factual source notes at the end of the book, where we also present in full the three documents that are indispensable for every American: the Declaration of Independence, the American Constitution with its Amendments, and the Emancipation Proclamation.

The thirty-eight Americans we have called to the witness stand represent more than two centuries of tumultuous history and unprecedented change. They include presidents, senators, writers, justices of the Supreme Court, political commentators, revolutionaries, and agitators. They represent America.

Now it is time to listen. The first one is already approaching the stand....

The Witnesses

1736–1799

PATRICK HENRY

ADDRESS BEFORE THE VIRGINIA
CONVENTION, MARCH 23, 1775

MR. PRESIDENT... this is no time for ceremony. The question before the house is one of awful moment to this country. For my own part I consider it as nothing less than a question of freedom or slavery.... If we wish to be free, if we mean to preserve inviolate those inestimable privileges for which we have been so long contending, if we mean not basely to abandon the noble struggle in which we have been so long engaged...we must fight!

Three millions of people, armed in the holy cause of liberty, and in such a country as that which we possess, are invincible by any force which our enemy can send against us....

Gentlemen may cry, Peace, Peace, but there is no peace.... Is life so dear or peace so sweet, as to be purchased at the price of chains and slavery? Forbid it, Almighty God! I know not what course others may take, but as for me, give me liberty or give me death!

★ ★ ★ ★

JOHN ADAMS

LETTER TO HIS WIFE, ABIGAIL,
MAY 17, 1776

A WHOLE government of our own choice, managed by persons whom we love, revere, and can confide in, has charms in it, for which men will fight.... In Charlestown when their new constitution was promulgated, and when their new Governor and Council and Assembly walked out in procession...they were beheld by the people with transports and tears of joy. The people gazed at them with a kind of rapture.... The reflection, that these were gentlemen whom they all loved, esteemed and revered, gentlemen of their own choice, whom they could trust, and whom they could displace, if any of them should behave amiss, affected them so that they could not help crying. They say, their people will never give up this government....

★　★　★　★

1735–1826

THOMAS McKEAN

*LETTER TO THE ASSOCIATORS OF
PENNSYLVANIA, JUNE 25, 1776*

YOU are not about to contend against the power of Great Britain, in order to displace one set of villains to make room for another.... You are about to contend for permanent freedom, to be supported by a government which will be derived from yourselves and which will have for its object, not the emolument of one man or class of men only, but the safety, liberty and happiness of every individual in the community....

The present campaign will probably decide the fate of America. It is now in your power to immortalize your names by mingling your achievements with the events of the year 1776—a year which, we hope, will be famed in the annals of history to the end of time, for establishing upon a lasting foundation the liberties of one-quarter of the globe.

★ ★ ★ ★

★ 1747–1820 ★

THE DECLARATION OF INDEPENDENCE

★ ★ ★ ★

JULY 4, 1776

WHEN in the course of human events it becomes necessary for one people to dissolve the political bands which have connected them with another, and to assume among the powers of the earth, the separate and equal station to which the Laws of Nature and of Nature's God entitle them, a decent respect to the opinions of mankind requires that they should declare the causes which impel them to the separation.

We hold these truths to be self-evident, that all men are created equal, that they are endowed by their Creator with certain unalienable Rights, that among these, are Life, Liberty, and the pursuit of Happiness—That, to secure these rights, Governments are instituted among Men, deriving their just powers from the consent of the governed—That, whenever any Form of Government becomes destructive of these ends, it is the Right of the People to alter or to abolish it, and to institute new Government, laying

The State House in Philadelphia

its foundation on such principles and organizing its powers in such form, as to them shall seem most likely to effect their Safety and Happiness....

1722–1803

SAMUEL ADAMS

*ADDRESS IN PHILADELPHIA AFTER THE
DECLARATION OF INDEPENDENCE,
AUGUST 1776*

OUR contest is not only whether we ourselves shall be free, but whether there shall be left to mankind an asylum on earth for civil and religious liberty.

This day presents the world with the most august spectacle its annals have ever unfolded—millions of freemen deliberately and voluntarily forming themselves into a society for their common defence and common happiness....

Other nations have received their laws from conquerors; some are indebted for a constitution to the sufferings of their ancestors through revolving centuries. The people of this country alone have formally and deliberately chosen a government for themselves, and with open and uninfluenced consent bound themselves to a social compact....

Our Union is now complete; our constitution composed, established and approved.... Be yourselves, O Americans, the authors of those laws on which your happiness depends!

1706–1790

Benjamin Franklin

LETTER TO CHARLES DE WEISSENSTEIN, 1778

THE body of our people are not merchants, but humble husbandmen, who delight in the cultivation of their lands.... We propose, if possible, to live in peace with all mankind.

LETTER TO JONATHAN SHIPLEY, 1786

WE are, I think, in the right road of improvement, for we are making experiments.... And I think we are daily more and more enlightened; so that I have no doubt of our obtaining in a few years as much public felicity, as good government is capable of offering.

AT THE CONSTITUTIONAL CONVENTION, 1787

WHEN you assemble a number of men, to have the advantage of their joint wisdom, you inevitably assemble with those men all their prejudices, their passions, their errors of opinion.... From such an assembly, can a *perfect* production be expected? It therefore astonishes me, Sir, to find this system approaching so near to perfection as it does.

THE CONSTITUTION

SEPTEMBER 17, 1787

WE, the people of the United States, in Order to form a more perfect Union, establish justice, insure domestic Tranquility, provide for the common defence, promote the general Welfare, and secure the Blessings of Liberty to ourselves and our Posterity, do ordain and establish this Constitution for the United States of America.

The Constitutional Convention

THE
BILL OF RIGHTS

1791

CONGRESS shall make no law... abridging the freedom of speech, or of the press; or the right of the people peaceably to assemble, and to petition the Government for a redress of their grievances....

The right of the people to be secure in their persons, houses, papers, and effects, against unreasonable searches and seizures, shall not be violated....

No person... shall be deprived of life, liberty, or property, without due process of law....

In all criminal prosecutions, the accused shall enjoy the right to a speedy and public trial... and to be informed of the nature and cause of the accusation... and to have the assistance of counsel for his defence....

The enumeration in the Constitution of certain rights shall not be construed to deny or disparage others retained by the people....

★ ★ ★ ★

1725–1792

16

GEORGE MASON

AT THE CONSTITUTIONAL CONVENTION,
1787

A BILL of rights, providing clearly and without the aid of sophisms for freedom of religion, freedom of the press, protection against standing armies, restriction against monopolies, the eternal and unremitting force of the habeas corpus laws, and trials by jury... a bill of rights is what the people are entitled to against every government on earth, general or particular, and what no just government should refuse, or rest on inference.

ON THE SLAVE TRADE, 1788

UNDER the royal government, this evil was looked upon as a great oppression, and many attempts were made to prevent it.... It was one of the great causes of our separation from Great Britain. Its exclusion has been a principal object of this state, and of most of the states in the union. The augmentation of slaves weakens the states; and such a trade is diabolical in itself, and disgraceful to mankind.

ALEXANDER HAMILTON

THE FEDERALIST, 1787

IT seems to have been reserved to the people of this country, by their conduct and example, to decide the important question, whether societies of men are really capable or not of establishing good government from reflection and choice, or whether they are forever destined to depend for their political constitutions on accident and force…. The crisis at which we are arrived may with propriety be regarded as the era in which that decision is to be made; and a wrong election of the part we shall act may, in this view, deserve to be considered as the general misfortune of mankind….

ON THE FEDERAL CONSTITUTION, 1788

THE true principle of government is this: make the system complete in its structure, give a perfect proportion and balance to its parts, and the powers you give it will never affect your security.

1755–1804

1745–1829

JOHN JAY

THE FEDERALIST, 1787

A STRONG sense of the value and blessings of union induced the people, at a very early period, to institute a federal government to preserve and perpetuate it....

I am persuaded in my own mind that the people have always thought right on this subject, and that their universal and uniform attachment to the cause of the Union rests on great and weighty reasons.

★ ★ ★ ★

CHISHOLM V. GEORGIA, 1793

THE people, in their collective and national capacity, established the present constitution. It is remarkable that in establishing it, the people exercised their own rights, and their own proper sovereignty, and conscious of the plenitude of it, they declared with becoming dignity, "We the people of the United States do ordain and establish this constitution." Here we see the people acting as sovereigns of the whole country.

THOMAS PAINE

THE RIGHTS OF MAN, 1790

THERE is one general principle that distinguishes freedom from slavery, which is, that all hereditary government over a people is to them a species of slavery, and reresentative government is freedom.

Man did not enter into society to become worse than he was before, nor to have fewer rights than he had before, but to have those rights better secured. His natural rights are the foundation of all his civil rights.

★　★　★　★

FROM a small spark kindled in America, a flame has arisen not to be extinguished. . . . It winds its progress from nation to nation, and conquers by a silent operation. Man finds himself changed, he scarcely perceives how. He acquires a knowledge of his rights by attending justly to his interest, and discovers in the event that the strength and powers of despotism consist wholly in the fear of resisting it, and that in order to be free, it is sufficient that he wills it.

1737–1809

1732–1799

GEORGE WASHINGTON

LETTER TO JAMES MADISON,
MAY 20, 1792

W E are all the children of the same country—a country great and rich in itself—capable and promising to be as prosperous and as happy as any the annals of history have ever brought to our view....

★ ★ ★ ★

T HE established government being the work of our own hands, with the seeds of amendment engrafted in the Constitution, may by wisdom, good disposition, and mutual allowances, aided by experience, bring it as near to perfection as any human institution ever approximated; and therefore the only struggle among us ought to be, who should be foremost in approximating, and finally accomplishing such great and desirable objects.

★ ★ ★ ★

1751–1836

JAMES MADISON

IN ANSWER TO "PACIFICUS,"
APRIL 22, 1793

IF there be a principle that ought not to be questioned within the United States, it is that every nation has a right to abolish an old government and establish a new one. This principle is not only recorded in every public archive, written in every American heart, and sealed with the blood of a host of American martyrs, but is the only lawful tenure by which the United States hold their existence as a nation.

★ ★ ★ ★

NATIONAL GAZETTE, FEBRUARY 20, 1792

A GOVERNMENT deriving its energy from the will of the society…is the government for which philosophy has been searching, and humanity has been fighting, from the most remote ages. Such are republican governments, which it is the glory of America to have invented and her unrivalled happiness to possess.

27

1743–1826

THOMAS JEFFERSON

LETTER TO WILLIAM GREEN MUMFORD,
JUNE 18, 1799

I CONSIDER man as formed for society, and endowed by nature with those dispositions which fit him for society. I believe also…that his mind is perfectible to a degree of which we cannot as yet form any conception…. Great fields are yet to be explored to which our faculties are equal, and that to an extent of which we cannot fix the limits….

To preserve the freedom of the human mind then and freedom of the press, every spirit should be ready to devote itself to martyrdom; for as long as we may think as we will, and speak as we think, the condition of man will proceed in improvement….

The generation which is going off the stage has deserved well of mankind for the struggles it has made, and for having arrested that course of despotism which has overwhelmed the world for thousands and thousands of years.

★   ★   ★   ★

JOHN MARSHALL

MARBURY V. MADISON, 1803

THAT the people have an original right to establish for their future government such principles as, in their opinion, shall most conduce to their own happiness is the basis on which the whole American fabric has been erected. The exercise of this original right is a very great exertion; nor can it, nor ought it, to be frequently repeated. The principles, therefore, so established are deemed fundamental. And as the authority from which they proceed is supreme, and can seldom act, they are designed to be permanent....

Certainly all those who have framed written constitutions contemplate them as forming the fundamental and paramount law of the nation and, consequently, the theory of every such government must be that an act of the legislature, repugnant to the constitution, is void.

This theory is essentially attached to a written constitution, and, is consequently, to be considered by this court, as one of the fundamental principles of our society.

★　★　★　★

1777–1852

HENRY CLAY

ADDRESS TO HOUSE OF REPRESENTATIVES,
"COMMITTEE OF THE WHOLE," MARCH 6, 1818

EVERY man who looks at the Constitution... must elevate his views to the height which this nation is destined to reach in the rank of nations. We are not legislating for this moment only, or for the present generation, or for the present populated limits of these States; but our acts must embrace a wider scope—reaching northwestwardly to the Pacific.... Imagine this extent of territory covered with sixty, or seventy, or an hundred millions of people....

ADDRESS TO HOUSE OF REPRESENTATIVES,
"COMMITTEE OF THE WHOLE," MAY 10, 1820

IT is in our power to create a system of which we shall be the center which would constitute the rallying point of human wisdom against all the despotism of the Old World.... Our institutions now make us free, but how long shall we continue so, if we mould our opinions on those of Europe?... Let us become real and true Americans, and place ourselves at the head of the American System.

JAMES MONROE

THE PEOPLE, THE SOVEREIGNS, 1825

A N enlightened and virtuous people, who are blessed with liberty, should look with profound attention to every occurrence which furnishes proof of the dangers to which that cause is exposed.... No people blessed with liberty could be deprived of it, if they were not made dupes and the instruments of their own destruction....

That a government founded on the sovereignty of the people with a wise organization and distribution of powers, is practicable over very extensive dominions and very populous communities, is certain, provided the state of society throws no impediment in its way....

The good people of these states have, therefore, been placed in a situation to make a fair experiment of the great problem, whether the people, as a people, are competent to self-government. All the circumstances with which they are blessed, more favorable to such a result than were ever enjoyed by any other people, impose on them, in like degree, the greater obligation to succeed.

1758–1831

1805–1859

ALEXIS DE TOCQUEVILLE

DEMOCRACY IN AMERICA, 1835

IN America the principle of the sovereignty of the people is neither barren nor concealed, as it is with some other nations; it is recognized by the customs and proclaimed by the laws; it spreads freely, and arrives without impediment at its most remote consequences. If there is a country in the world where the doctrine of the sovereignty of the people can be fairly appreciated, where it can be studied in its application to the affairs of society, and where its dangers and advantages may be judged, that country is assuredly America.

★ ★ ★ ★

IN examining the Constitution of the United States, which is the most perfect federal constitution that ever existed, one is startled at the variety of information and the amount of discernment that it presupposes in the people whom it is meant to govern.

1767–1845

ANDREW JACKSON

MESSAGE TO CONGRESS, JULY 10, 1832

DISTINCTIONS in society will always exist under every just government. Equality of talents, of education, or of wealth can not be produced by human institutions. In the full enjoyment of the gifts of Heaven and the fruits of superior industry, economy, and virtue, every man is equally entitled to protection by law; but when the laws undertake to add to these natural and just advantages artificial distinctions, to grant titles, gratuities and exclusive privileges, to make the rich richer and the potent more powerful, the humble members of society... have a right to complain of the injustice of their Government. There are no necessary evils in Government. Its evils exist only in its abuses....

Experience should teach us wisdom. Most of the difficulties our government now encounters and most of the dangers which impend over our Union have sprung from an abandonment of the legitimate objects of government by our national legislation.... It is time to pause in our career to review our principles.

JOHN QUINCY ADAMS

DIARY, MARCH 3, 1820

I T is among the evils of slavery that it taints the very sources of moral principle.... The bargain between freedom and slavery contained in the Constitution of the United States is morally and politically vicious, inconsistent with the principles upon which alone our revolution can be justified; cruel and oppressive, by riveting the chains of slavery, by pledging the faith of freedom to maintain and perpetuate the tyranny of the master; and grossly unequal and impolitic, by admitting that slaves are at once enemies to be kept in subjection, property to be secured or restored to their owners, and persons not to be represented themselves, but for whom their masters are privileged with nearly a double share of representation. The consequence has been that this slave representation has governed the Union.... If the Union must be dissolved, slavery is precisely the question upon which it ought to break.

★ ★ ★ ★

1767–1848

ALBERT GALLATIN

PEACE WITH MEXICO, 1847

THE people of the United States have been placed by Providence in a position never before enjoyed by any other nation.... They found themselves, at the epoch of their independence, in full enjoyment of religious, civil, and political liberty...natural rights for which the people of other countries have for a long time contended and still do contend. They were, and you still are the supreme sovereigns.... For the proper exercise of such uncontrolled powers and privileges, you are responsible to posterity....

Your forefathers, the founders of the Republic, imbued with a deep feeling of their rights and duties, did not deviate from these principles....

At present, all these principles would seem to have been abandoned. The most just, a purely defensive war—and no other is justifiable—is necessarily attended with a train of great and unavoidable evils. What shall we say of one, iniquitous in its origin, and provoked by ourselves, of a war of aggression, which is now publicly avowed to be one of intended conquest?

1761–1849

1817–1862

HENRY DAVID THOREAU

ON THE DUTY OF CIVIL DISOBEDIENCE,
1849

ALL men recognize the right of revolution; that is, the right to refuse allegiance to and to resist the government, when its tyranny or its inefficiency are great and unendurable....

When a sixth of the population of a nation which has undertaken to be the refuge of liberty are slaves, and a whole country is unjustly overrun and conquered by a foreign army, and subjected to military law, I think that it is not too soon for honest men to rebel and revolutionize. What makes this duty the more urgent is the fact, that the country so overrun is not our own, but ours is the invading army....

There are thousands who are *in opinion* opposed to slavery and to the war [with Mexico], who yet in effect do nothing to put an end to them....

It is not a man's duty, as a matter of course, to devote himself to the eradication of any, even the most enormous wrong... but it is his duty... not to give it practically his support.

1782–1852

DANIEL WEBSTER

MESSAGE TO CONGRESS,
MARCH 7, 1850

MR. President, I wish to speak today, not as a Massachusetts man, not as a northern man, but as an American, and as a member of the Senate of the United States.... I hear with pain, and anguish, and distress, the word secession.... Why, what would be the result?... Where is the line to be drawn? What is to remain American? What am I to be?—an American no longer? Where is the flag of the Republic to remain?... Why, sir, our ancestors—our fathers and our grandfathers, those of them that are yet living among us with prolonged lives—would rebuke and reproach us; and our children and grandchildren would cry out, Shame upon us!, if we, of this generation should dishonor these ensigns of the power of the Government, and the harmony of the Union, which is every day felt among us with so much joy and gratitude....

Never did there devolve, on any generation of men, higher trusts than now devolve upon us for the preservation of this Constitution, and the harmony and peace of all who are destined to live under it.

JAMES BUCHANAN

MESSAGE TO CONGRESS,
DECEMBER 3, 1860

BUT may I be permitted solemnly to invoke my countrymen to pause and deliberate before they determine to destroy this the grandest temple which has ever been dedicated to human freedom since the world began? It has been consecrated by the blood of our fathers, by the glories of the past, and by the hopes of the future. The Union has already made us the most prosperous, and ere long will, if preserved, render us the most powerful, nation on the face of the earth.… Surely when we reach the brink of the yawning abyss we shall recoil with horror from the last fatal plunge.

By such a dread catastrophe the hopes of the friends of freedom throughout the world would be destroyed, and a long night of leaden despotism would enshroud the nations. Our example for more than eighty years would not only be lost, but it would be quoted as a conclusive proof that man is unfit for self-government.

★　★　★　★

1791–1868

WALT WHITMAN

THE EIGHTEENTH PRESIDENCY!, 1856

T HE times are full of great portents in These States and in the Whole world. Freedom against slavery is not issuing here alone, but is issuing everywhere.... Everything indicates unparalleled reforms. Races are marching and countermarching by swift millions and tens of millions. Never was justice so mighty among injustice; never did the idea of equality erect itself so haughty and uncompromising amid inequality, as to-day....

What whispers are these running through the eastern continents, and crossing the Atlantic and Pacific? What historical denouements are these we are approaching? On all sides tyrants tremble, crowns are unsteady, the human race restive, on the watch for some better era, some divine war. No man knows what will happen next, but all know that some such things are to happen as mark the greatest moral convulsions of the earth. Who shall play the hand for America in these tremendous games?

★ ★ ★ ★

★   ★

1819–1892

★   ★

1809–1865

ABRAHAM LINCOLN

GETTYSBURG ADDRESS,
NOVEMBER 19, 1863

FOURSCORE and seven years ago our fathers brought forth on this continent a new nation, conceived in liberty and dedicated to the proposition that all men are created equal.

Now we are engaged in a great civil war testing whether that nation, or any nation so conceived and so dedicated, can long endure. We are met on a great battlefield of that war. We have come to dedicate a portion of that field as a final resting-place for those who here gave their lives that that nation might live. It is altogether fitting and proper that we should do this.

But, in a larger sense, we cannot dedicate, we cannot consecrate, we cannot hallow this ground. The brave men, living and dead, who struggled here have consecrated it far above our poor power to add or detract.... It is rather for us to be here dedicated to the great task remaining before us.... We here highly resolve that these dead shall not have died in vain, that this nation under God shall have a new birth of freedom, and that government of the people, by the people, for the people shall not perish from the earth.

★ ★

1822–1885

★ ★

ULYSSES S. GRANT

MEMOIRS, 1884

OUR republican institutions were regarded as experiments up to the breaking out of the rebellion, and monarchical Europe generally believed that our republic was a rope of sand that would part the moment the slightest strain was brought upon it. Now it has shown itself capable of dealing with one of the greatest wars that was ever made, and our people have proven themselves to be the most formidable in war of any nationality....

But the war between the States was a very bloody and costly war. One side or the other had to yield principles they deemed dearer than life before it could be brought to an end....

The war has made us a nation of great power and intelligence. We have but little to do to preserve peace, happiness and prosperity at home, and the respect of other nations. Our experience ought to teach us the necessity of the first; our power secures the latter.

★   ★   ★   ★

RALPH WALDO EMERSON

ON THE EMANCIPATION PROCLAMATION, 1862

A DAY which most of us dared not hope to see, an event worth the dreadful war, worth its costs and uncertainties, now seems to be close before us....

This act makes that the lives of our heroes have not been sacrificed in vain. It makes a victory of our defeats. Our hurts are healed; the health of the nation is repaired.... With this blot removed from our national honor, we shall not fear henceforth to show our faces among mankind.

*ADDRESS TO THE MERCANTILE LIBRARY
ASSOCIATION OF BOSTON, 1844*

WE cannot look on the freedom of this country, in connexion with its youth, without a presentiment that here shall laws and institutions exist on some scale of proportion to the majesty of nature. To men legislating for the vast area betwixt the snows and the tropics, something of the gravity and grandeur of nature will infuse itself into the code....

1803–1882

DAVID DAVIS

EX PARTE MILLIGAN, 1866

THE Constitution of the United States is a law for rulers and people, equally in war and in peace, and covers with the shield of its protection all classes of men, at all times, and under all circumstances. No doctrine involving more pernicious consequences was ever invented by the wit of man than that any of its provisions can be suspended during any of the great exigencies of government. Such a doctrine leads directly to anarchy or despotism.... The government, within the Constitution, has all the powers granted to it which are necessary to preserve its existence....

The illustrious men who framed that instrument were guarding the foundations of civil liberty against the abuses of unlimited power; they were full of wisdom, and the lessons of history informed them that a trial by an established court, assisted by an impartial jury, was the only sure way of protecting the citizens against oppression and wrong.

★ ★ ★ ★

★ ★

1815–1886

★ ★

SUSAN B. ANTHONY

ADDRESS IN MONROE COUNTY,
NEW YORK, 1872

WHEN... people enter into a free government, they do not barter away their natural rights; they simply pledge themselves to protect each other in the enjoyment of them through prescribed judicial and legislative tribunals. They agree to abandon the methods of brute force in the adjustment of their differences and adopt those of civilization.... The Declaration of Independence, the United States Constitution... propose to protect the people in the exercise of their God-given rights. Not one of them pretends to bestow rights....

It was we, the people, not we the white male citizens, nor we, the male citizens; but we, the whole people who formed this Union. We formed it not to give the blessings of liberty, but to secure them; not to the half of ourselves and half of our posterity, but to the whole people, women as well as men.

No barriers whatever stand today between women and the exercise of their right to vote, save those of precedent and prejudice....

1820–1906

1817–1895

FREDERICK DOUGLASS

ADDRESS TO COMMEMORATE THE
TWENTY-THIRD ANNIVERSARY OF THE
EMANCIPATION PROCLAMATION, 1885

WHAT rocks Europe today? What causes the Emperor of all the Russias to be uneasy on his pillow? What makes Austria tremble? Why does England start up frantically at midnight and search her premises? You know, and I know, that these countries have aggrieved classes among them who have just ground for complaint against their governments.

All the world is a school, and in it one lesson is just now being taught, and that is the utter insecurity of life and property in the presence of an aggrieved class. This lesson can be learned by the ignorant as well as by the wise.

Education, the sheet anchor of safety to a society where liberty and justice are secure, is a dangerous thing to society in the presence of injustice and oppression....

Let not my words be construed as a menace, but taken as I mean them—as a warning.

★   ★

1858–1919

★   ★

THEODORE ROOSEVELT

OUTLOOK, JANUARY 21, 1910

THE existence of this nation has no real significance from the standpoint of humanity at large, unless it means the rule of the people and the achievement of a greater measure of widely diffused popular well-being than has ever before obtained on a like scale.

ADDRESS AT CARNEGIE HALL, NEW YORK, MARCH 20, 1912

THE worth of our great experiment depends upon its being in good faith an experiment—the first that has ever been tried—in true democracy on the scale of a continent, on a scale as vast as that of the mightiest empires of the Old World.

FOURTH ANNUAL MESSAGE, DECEMBER 4, 1904

FREEDOM is not a gift that tarries long in the hands of cowards…. The eternal vigilance which is the price of liberty must be exercised sometimes to guard against outside foes…. A great free people owes it to itself and to all mankind not to sink into helplessness before the powers of evil.

WOODROW WILSON

MESSAGE TO CONGRESS, APRIL 2, 1917

IT is a fearful thing to lead this great and peaceful people into war, into the most terrible and disastrous of all wars, civilization itself seeming to be in the balance. But the right is more precious than peace, and we shall fight for the things which we have always carried nearest our hearts—for democracy, for the right of those who submit to authority to have a voice in their own governments, for the rights and liberties of small nations, for a universal domination of right by such a concert of free peoples as shall bring peace and safety to all nations and make the world itself at last free. To such a task we can dedicate our lives and our fortunes, everything that we are and everything that we have, with the pride of those who know that the day has come when America is privileged to spend her blood and her might for the principles that gave her birth and happiness and the peace which she has treasured. God helping her, she can do no other.

★　★　★　★

1856–1924

1856–1941

LOUIS BRANDEIS

ON FREEDOM OF EXPRESSION, 1927

THOSE who won our independence believed that the final end of the state was to make men free to develop their faculties.... They valued liberty both as an end and as a means. They believed liberty to be the secret of happiness and courage to be the secret of liberty;... that public discussion is a political duty; and that this should be the fundamental principle of the American government.

Fear of serious injury cannot alone justify suppression of free speech and assembly.... It is the function of speech to free men from the bondage of irrational fears.

Those who won our independence by revolution were not cowards. They did not fear political change. They did not exalt order at the cost of liberty. To courageous, self-reliant men, with confidence in the power of free and fearless reasoning applied through the processes of popular government, no danger flowing from speech may be termed clear and present.... Such, in my opinion, is the command of the Constitution.

★ ★ ★ ★

FRANKLIN DELANO ROOSEVELT

ADDRESS, MAY 26, 1940

FOR more than three centuries we Americans have been building on this continent a free society, a society in which the promise of the human spirit may find fulfillment. Commingled here are the blood and genius of all the peoples of the world who have sought this promise.

MESSAGE TO CONGRESS, JANUARY 1, 1939

THERE comes a time in the affairs of men when they must prepare to defend, not their homes alone, but the tenets… on which their governments and their very civilization are founded.

THIRD INAUGURAL ADDRESS, JANUARY 20, 1941

DEMOCRACY alone has constructed an unlimited civilization capable of infinite progress in the improvement of human life… for it is the most humane, the most advanced and in the end the most unconquerable of all forms of human society.

1882–1945

HARRY TRUMAN

RADIO ADDRESS, AUGUST 9, 1945

OUR victory in Europe was more than a victory of arms. It was the victory of one way of life over another. It was a victory of an ideal founded on the rights of the common man, on the dignity of the human being....

The war has shown us that we have tremendous resources to make all the materials for war. It has shown us that we have skillful workers and managers and able generals, and a brave people capable of bearing arms.

All these things we knew before.

The new thing—the thing we had not known —the thing we have learned now and never should forget, is this: that a society of self-governing men is more powerful, more enduring, more creative than any other kind of society, however disciplined, however centralized.

We know now that the basic proposition of the worth and dignity of man... is the strongest, the most creative force now present in the world.

★ ★ ★ ★

1884–1972

1889–1974

WALTER LIPPMANN

THE AMERICAN DESTINY, 1945

FATE has brought it about that America is at the center, no longer on the edges, of Western civilization. In this fact resides the American destiny. We can deny the fact and refuse our destiny. If we do, Western civilization, which is the glory of our world, will become a disorganized and decaying fringe.... But if we comprehend our destiny we shall become equal to it. The vision is there and our people need not perish.

For America is now called to do what the founders and pioneers always believed was the American task: to make the New World a place where the ancient faith can flourish anew, and its eternal promise at last be redeemed. To ask whether the American nation will rise to this occasion and be equal to its destiny is to ask whether Americans have the will to live....

This, I believe, is the prophecy which events announce. Whether we now hear it gladly or shrink away from it suspiciously, it will yet come to pass.

★ ★ ★ ★

1902–1998

HENRY STEELE COMMAGER

"WHO IS LOYAL TO AMERICA?," 1947

I F our democracy is to flourish it must have criticism, if our government is to function it must have dissent. Only totalitarian governments insist upon conformity and they—as we know—do so at their peril.... Americans have a stake in nonconformity, for they know that the American genius is nonconformist.

It is easier to say what loyalty is not than to say what it is. It is not conformity. It is not passive acquiescence in the status quo.... It is a tradition, an ideal, and a principle.... It is a realization that America was born of revolt, flourished on dissent, became great through experimentation....

From the beginning Americans have known that there were new worlds to conquer, new truths to be discovered. Every effort to confine Americanism to a single pattern, to constrain it to a single formula, is disloyalty to everything that is valid in Americanism.

★ ★ ★ ★

JOHN F. KENNEDY

INAUGURAL ADDRESS, JANUARY 20, 1961

WE observe today not a victory of a party, but a celebration of freedom.... For I have sworn before you and Almighty God the same solemn oath our forebears prescribed nearly a century and three-quarters ago.

The world is very different now.... And yet the same revolutionary beliefs for which our forefathers fought are still at issue around the globe—the belief that the rights of man come not from the generosity of the state but from the hand of God.

We dare not forget today that we are the heirs of that first revolution. Let the word go forth from this time and place, to friend and foe alike, that the torch has been passed to a new generation of Americans—born in this century, tempered by war, disciplined by a hard and bitter peace, proud of our ancient heritage.... Let every nation, whether it wishes us well or ill know we shall pay any price, bear any burden, meet any hardship, support any friend, oppose any foe, in order to assure the survival and the success of liberty.

★ ★ ★ ★

1917–1963

MARTIN LUTHER KING, JR.

*ADDRESS AT LINCOLN MEMORIAL,
AUGUST 28, 1963*

I SAY to you today, my friends, that in spite of the difficulties and frustrations of the moment I still have a dream…. It is a dream deeply rooted in the American dream. I have a dream that one day this nation will rise up and live out the true meaning of its creed: "We hold these truths to be self-evident, that all men are created equal." I have a dream that one day on the red hills of Georgia the sons of the former slaves and the sons of the former slaveowners will be able to sit down together at the table of brotherhood. I have a dream that my four little children will one day live in a nation where they will not be judged by the color of their skin but by the content of their character.

I have a dream today…. With this faith we will be able to hew out of the mountain of despair a stone of hope….

And if America is to be a great nation this must become true.

★　★　★　★

★ 1929–1968 ★

MADELEINE K. ALBRIGHT

*SUSTAINING DEMOCRACY IN THE
TWENTY-FIRST CENTURY, JANUARY 18, 2000*

DEMOCRACY is the hard rock upon which America's world leadership is built. It is why our land has attracted to its shores a steady stream of the world's boldest and most creative women and men. It is why our predecessors had the courage and faith to triumph in two global conflicts. It is why we were able to stand tall during the decades of the Cold War.

We know, from our own turbulent history, that the path to democracy is rocky, treacherous, and always uphill. But we also know that if we keep faith with the democratic principles that have guided us this far, we will have the light we need to guide us through the perilous miles to come.

★ ★ ★ ★

1937–

*D*OCUMENTS

IN CONGRESS, JULY 4, 1776

THE UNANIMOUS DECLARATION OF THE THIRTEEN UNITED STATES OF AMERICA

When in the Course of human events, it becomes necessary for one people to dissolve the political bands which have connected them with another, and to assume among the powers of the earth, the separate and equal station to which the Laws of Nature and of Nature's God entitle them, a decent respect to the opinions of mankind requires that they should declare the causes which impel them to the separation.

We hold these truths to be self-evident, that all men are created equal, that they are endowed by their Creator with certain unalienable Rights, that among these, are Life, Liberty, and the pursuit of Happiness.—That, to secure these rights, Governments are instituted among Men, deriving their just Powers from the consent of the governed.—That, whenever any Form of Government becomes destructive of these ends, it is the Right of the People to alter or to abolish it, and to institute new Government, laying its foundation on such principles, and organizing its powers in such form, as to them shall seem most likely to effect their Safety and Happiness. Prudence, indeed, will dictate that Governments long established should not be changed for light and transient causes—and, accordingly, all experience hath shewn, that mankind are more disposed to suffer, while evils are sufferable, than to right themselves by abolishing the forms to which they are accustomed. But when a long train of abuses and usurpations, pursuing invariably the same Object evinces a design to reduce them under absolute Despotism, it is their right, it is their duty, to throw off such Government, and to provide new Guards for their future Security.—Such has been the patient sufferance of these Colonies; and such is now the necessity which constrains them to alter their former Systems of Government. The history of the present King of Great Britain is a history of repeated injuries and usurpations, all having in direct object the establishment of an absolute Tyranny over these States. To prove this, let Facts be submitted to a candid world.

He has refused his Assent to Laws, the most wholesome and necessary for the public good.

He has forbidden his Governors to pass Laws of immediate and pressing importance, unless suspended in their operation till his Assent should be obtained; and when so suspended, he has utterly neglected to attend to them.

He has refused to pass other Laws for the accommodation of large districts of people, unless those people would relinquish the right of Representation in the legislature; a right inestimable to them and formidable to tyrants only.

He has called together legislative bodies at places unusual, uncomfortable, and distant from the depository of their Public Records, for the sole purpose of fatiguing them into compliance with his measures.

He has dissolved Representative Houses repeatedly, for opposing with manly firmness his invasions on the rights of the people.

He has refused for a long time, after such dissolutions, to cause others to be elected; whereby the Legislative Powers, incapable of Annihilation, have returned to the People at large for their exercise; the State remaining in the mean time exposed to all the dangers of invasion from without, and convulsions within.

He has endeavoured to prevent the population of these States; for that purpose obstructing the Laws for Naturalization of Foreigners; refusing to pass others to encourage their migrations hither, and raising the conditions of new Appropriations of Lands.

He has obstructed the Administration of Justice, by refusing his Assent to Laws for establishing Judiciary Powers.

He has made Judges dependent on his Will alone, for the tenure of their offices, and the amount and payment of their salaries.

He has erected a multitude of New Offices, and sent hither swarms of Officers to harrass our people, and eat out their substance.

He has kept among us, in times of peace, Standing Armies, without the Consent of our legislatures.

He has affected to render the Military independent of and superior to the Civil Power.

He has combined with others to subject us to a jurisdiction foreign to our constitution, and unacknowledged by our laws; giving his Assent to their Acts of pretended Legislation:

For quartering large bodies of armed troops among us:

For protecting them, by a mock Trial, from punishment for any murders which they should commit on the Inhabitants of these States:

For cutting off our Trade with all parts of the world:

For imposing Taxes on us without our Consent:

For depriving us in many cases, of the benefits of Trial by Jury:

For transporting us beyond Seas to be tried for pretended offenses:

For abolishing the free System of English Laws in a neighbouring Province, establishing therein an Arbitrary government, and enlarging its Boundaries, so as to render it at once an example and fit instrument for introducing the same absolute rule into these Colonies:

For taking away our Charters, abolishing our most valuable Laws and altering fundamentally the Forms of our Governments:

For suspending our own Legislatures, and declaring themselves invested with Power to legislate for us in all cases whatsoever.

He has abdicated Government here, by declaring us out of his protection and waging War against us.

He has plundered our seas, ravaged our Coasts, burnt our towns, and destroyed the lives of our people.

He is at this time transporting large Armies of foreign Mercenaries to compleat the works of death, desolation and tyranny, already begun with circumstances of Cruelty & Perfidy scarcely paralleled in the most barbarous ages, and totally unworthy the Head of a civilized nation.

He has constrained our fellow Citizens taken Captive on the high Seas to bear Arms against their Country, to become the executioners of their friends and Brethren, or to fall themselves by their Hands.

He has excited domestic insurrections amongst us, and has endeavoured to bring on the inhabitants of our frontiers, the merciless Indian Savages, whose known rule of warfare, is an undistinguished destruction of all ages, sexes and conditions.

In every stage of these Oppressions We have Petitioned for Redress in the most humble terms: Our repeated Petitions have been answered only by repeated injury. A Prince, whose character is thus marked by every act which may define a Tyrant, is unfit to be the ruler of a free people.

Nor have We been wanting in attentions to our British

brethren. We have warned them from time to time of attempts by their legislature to extend an unwarrantable jurisdiction over us. We have reminded them of the circumstances of our emigration and settlement here. We have appealed to their native justice and magnanimity, and we have conjured them by the ties of our common kindred to disavow these usurpations, which, would inevitably interrupt our connections and correspondence. They too have been deaf to the voice of justice and of consanguinity. We must, therefore, acquiesce in the necessity, which denounces our Separation, and hold them, as we hold the rest of mankind, Enemies in War, in Peace Friends.

WE, THEREFORE, the Representatives of the UNITED STATES OF AMERICA, in General Congress, Assembled, appealing to the Supreme Judge of the World for the rectitude of our intentions, do, in the Name, and by Authority of the good People of these Colonies, solemnly publish and declare, That these United Colonies are, and of Right ought to be FREE AND INDEPENDENT STATES; that they are Absolved from all Allegiance to the British Crown, and that all political connexion between them and the State of Great Britain, is and ought to be totally dissolved; and that, as free and independent states, they have full Power to levy War, conclude Peace, contract Alliances, establish Commerce, and to do all other Acts and Things which independent states may of right do.—And for the support of this Declaration, with a firm reliance on the protection of Divine Providence, we mutually pledge to each other our Lives, our Fortunes, and our sacred Honour.

John Adams	Lyman Hall	Francis Lewis
Samuel Adams	John Hancock	Philip Livingston
Josiah Bartlett	Benjamin Harrison	Thomas Lynch, Jr.
Carter Braxton	John Hart	Thomas McKean
Charles Carroll	Joseph Hewes	Arthur Middleton
Samuel Chase	Thomas Heyward Jr.	Lewis Morris
Abraham Clark	William Hooper	Robert Morris
George Clymer	Stephen Hopkins	John Morton
William Ellery	Francis Hopkinson	Thomas Nelson, Jr.
William Floyd	Sam'el Huntington	William Paca
Benjamin Franklin	Thomas Jefferson	Robert Treat Paine
Elbridge Gerry	Richard Henry Lee	John Penn
Button Gwinnett	Francis Lightfoot Lee	George Read

Caesar Rodney
George Ross
Benjamin Rush
Edward Rutledge
Roger Sherman
James Smith

Richard Stockton
Thomas Stone
George Taylor
Matthew Thornton
George Walton
William Whipple

William Williams
James Wilson
John Witherspoon
Oliver Wolcott
George Wythe

THE CONSTITUTION OF THE UNITED STATES OF AMERICA

We the People of the United States, in Order to form a more perfect Union, establish Justice, insure domestic Tranquility, provide for the common defence, promote the general Welfare, and secure the Blessings of Liberty to ourselves and our Posterity, do ordain and establish this Constitution for the United States of America.

ARTICLE. I.

SECTION. 1. All legislative Powers herein granted shall be vested in a Congress of the United States, which shall consist of a Senate and House of Representatives.

SECTION. 2. The House of Representatives shall be composed of Members chosen every second Year by the People of the several States, and the Electors in each State shall have the Qualifications requisite for Electors of the most numerous Branch of the State Legislature.

No Person shall be a Representative who shall not have attained to the Age of twenty five Years, and been seven Years a Citizen of the United States, and who shall not, when elected, be an Inhabitant of that State in which he shall be chosen.

[Representatives and direct Taxes shall be apportioned among the several States which may be included within this Union, according to their respective Numbers, which shall be determined by adding to the whole Number of free Persons, including those bound to Service for a term of Years, and excluding Indians not taxed, three fifths of all other Persons.]*

The actual Enumeration shall be made within three Years after the first Meeting of the Congress of the United States, and

[Note: The Constitution and all amendments are presented in their original form. Items which have since been amended or superseded, as underlined in the footnotes, are bracketed.]

* Changed by clause section 2 of the fourteenth amendment.

within every subsequent Term of ten Years, in such Manner as they shall by Law direct. The number of Representatives shall not exceed one for every thirty Thousand,* but each State shall have at Least one Representative; and until such enumeration shall be made, the State of New Hampshire shall be entitled to chuse three, Massachusetts eight, Rhode-Island and Providence Plantations one, Connecticut five, New York six, New Jersey four, Pennsylvania eight, Delaware one, Maryland six, Virginia ten, North Carolina five, South Carolina five, and Georgia three.

When vacancies happen in the Representation from any State, the Executive Authority thereof shall issue Writs of Election to fill such Vacancies.

The House of Representatives shall chuse their Speaker and other Officers; and shall have the sole Power of Impeachment.

SECTION. 3. The Senate of the United States shall be composed of two Senators from each State, [chosen by the Legislalure thereof,]** for six Years; and each Senator shall have one Vote.

Immediately after they shall be assembled in Consequence of the first Election, they shall be divided as equally as may be into three Classes. The Seats of the Senators of the first Class shall be vacated at the Expiration of the second Year, of the second Class at the Expiration of the fourth Year, and of the third Class at the expiration of the sixth Year, so that one third may be chosen every second Year; [and if Vacancies happen by Resignation, or otherwise, during the Recess of the Legislature of any State, the Executive thereof may make temporary Appointments until the next Meeting of the Legislature, which shall then fill such Vacancies.]***

No Person shall be a Senator who shall not have attained to the Age of thirty Years, and been nine Years a Citizen of the United States, and who shall not, when elected, be an Inhabitant of that State for which he shall be chosen.

The Vice President of the United States shall be President of the Senate, but shall have no Vote, unless they be equally divided.

The Senate shall chuse their other Officers, and also a President pro tempore, in the Absence of the Vice President, or when he shall exercise the Office of President of the United States.

* Ratio in 1965 was one to over 410,100.
** Changed by the seventeenth amendment.
***Changed by the seventeenth amendment.

The Senate shall have the sole Power to try all Impeachments. When sitting for that Purpose, they shall be on Oath or Affirmation. When the President of the United States is tried, the Chief Justice shall preside: And no Person shall be convicted without the Concurrence of two thirds of the Members present.

Judgment in Cases of Impeachment shall not extend further than to removal from Office, and disqualification to hold and enjoy any Office of honor, Trust or Profit under the United States: but the Party convicted shall nevertheless be liable and subject to Indictment, Trial, Judgment and Punishment, according to law.

SECTION. 4. The Times, Places and Manner of holding Elections for Senators and Representatives, shall be prescribed in each State by the Legislature thereof; but the Congress may at any time by Law make or alter such Regulations, except as to the Place of chusing Senators.

The Congress shall assemble at least once in every Year, and such Meeting shall be [on the first Monday in December,]* unless they shall by Law appoint a different Day.

SECTION. 5. Each House shall be the Judge of the Elections, Returns and Qualifications of its own Members, and a Majority of each shall constitute a Quorum to do Business; but a smaller Number may adjourn from day to day, and may be authorized to compel the Attendance of absent Members, in such Manner, and under such Penalties as each House may provide.

Each House may determine the Rules of its Proceedings, punish its Members for disorderly Behaviour, and, with the Concurrence of two thirds, expel a Member.

Each House shall keep a Journal of its Proceedings, and from time to time publish the same, excepting such Parts as may in their Judgment require Secrecy; and the Yeas and Nays of the Members of either House on any question shall, at the Desire of one fifth of those Present, be entered on the Journal.

Neither House, during the Session of Congress, shall, without the Consent of the other, adjourn for more than three days, nor to any other Place than that in which the two Houses shall be sitting.

SECTION. 6. The Senators and Representatives shall receive a Compensation for their Services, to be ascertained by Law, and

*Changed by section 2 of the twentieth amendment.

paid out of the Treasury of the United States. They shall in all Cases, except Treason, Felony and Breach of the Peace, be privileged from Arrest during their Attendance at the Session of their respective Houses, and in going to and returning from the same; and for any Speech or Debate in either House, they shall not be questioned in any other Place.

No Senator or Representative shall, during the Time for which he was elected, be appointed to any civil Office under the Authority of the United States, which shall have been created, or the Emoluments whereof shall have been encreased during such time; and no Person holding any office under the United States, shall be a Member of either House during his Continuance in Office.

SECTION. 7. All Bills for raising Revenue shall originate in the House of Representatives; but the Senate may propose or concur with Amendments as on other Bills.

Every Bill which shall have passed the House of Representatives and the Senate, shall, before it becomes a Law, be presented to the President of the United States; If he approve he shall sign it, but if not he shall return it, with his Objections to that House in which it shall have originated, who shall enter the Objections at large on their Journal, and proceed to reconsider it. If after such Reconsideration two thirds of that House shall agree to pass the Bill, it shall be sent, together with the Objections, to the other House, by which it shall likewise be reconsidered, and if approved by two thirds of that House, it shall become a Law. But in all such Cases the Votes of both Houses shall be determined by Yeas and Nays, and the Names of the Persons voting for and against the Bill shall be entered on the Journal of each House respectively. If any Bill shall not be returned by the President within ten Days (Sundays excepted) after it shall have been presented to him, the Same shall be a Law, in like Manner as if he had signed it, unless the Congress by their Adjournment prevent its Return, in which Case it shall not be a Law.

Every Order, Resolution, or Vote to which the Concurrence of the Senate and House of Representatives may be necessary (except on a question of Adjournment) shall be presented to the President of the United States; and before the Same shall take Effect, shall be approved by him, or being disapproved by him, shall be repassed by two thirds of the Senate and House of Representatives, according to the Rules and Limitations prescribed in the Case of a Bill.

SECTION. 8. The Congress shall have Power to lay and collect Taxes, Duties, Imposts and Excises, to pay the Debts and provide for the common Defence and general Welfare of the United States; but all Duties, Imposts and Excises shall be uniform throughout the United States;

To borrow money on the credit of the United States;

To regulate Commerce with foreign Nations, and among the several States, and with the Indian Tribes;

To establish an uniform Rule of Naturalization, and uniform Laws on the subject of Bankruptcies throughout the United States;

To coin Money, regulate the Value thereof, and of foreign Coin, and fix the Standard of Weights and Measures;

To provide for the Punishment of counterfeiting the Securities and current Coin of the United States;

To establish Post Offices and post Roads;

To promote the Progress of Science and useful Arts, by securing for limited Times to Authors and Inventors the exclusive Right to their respective Writings and Discoveries;

To constitute Tribunals inferior to the supreme Court;

To define and punish Piracies and Felonies committed on the high Seas, and offenses against the Law of Nations;

To declare War, grant Letters of Marque and Reprisal, and make Rules concerning Captures on Land and Water;

To raise and support Armies, but no Appropriation of Money to that Use shall be for a longer term than two Years;

To provide and maintain a Navy;

To make Rules for the Government and Regulation of the land and naval Forces;

To provide for calling forth the Militia to execute the Laws of the Union, suppress Insurrections and repel Invasions;

To provide for organizing, arming, and disciplining, the Militia, and for governing such Part of them as may be employed in the Service of the United States, reserving to the States respectively, the Appointment of the officers, and the Authority of training the Militia according to the discipline prescribed by Congress;

To exercise exclusive Legislation in all Cases whatsoever, over such District (not exceeding ten Miles square) as may, by Cession of particular States, and the Acceptance of Congress, become the Seat of the Government of the United States, and to exercise like Authority over all Places purchased by the Consent of the Legislature of the State in which the Same shall be, for the Erection of Forts, Magazines, Arsenals, dock-Yards, and other needful Buildings;—And

To make all Laws which shall be necessary and proper tor carrying into Execution the foregoing Powers, and all other Powers vested by this Constitution in the Government of the United States, or in any Department or Officer thereof.

SECTION. 9. The Migration or Importation of such Persons as any of the States now existing shall think proper to admit, shall not be prohibited by the Congress prior to the Year one thousand eight hundred and eight, but a Tax or duty may be imposed on such Importation, not exceeding ten dollars for each Person.

The Privilege of the Writ of Habeas Corpus shall not be suspended, unless when in Cases of Rebellion or Invasion the public Safety may require it.

No Bill of Attainder or ex post facto law shall be passed.

No Capitation, or other direct, Tax shall be laid, unless in Proportion to the Census or Enumeration herein before directed to be taken.*

No Tax or Duty shall be laid on Articles exported from any State.

No Preference shall be given by any Regulation of Commerce or Revenue to the Ports of one State over those of another: nor shall Vessels bound to, or from, one State, be obliged to enter, clear, or pay Duties in another.

No Money shall be drawn from the Treasury, but in Consequence of Appropriations made by Law; and a regular Statement and Account of the Receipts and Expenditures of all public Money shall be published from time to time.

No Title of Nobility shall be granted by the United States: And no Person holding any Office of Profit or Trust under them, shall, without the Consent of the Congress, accept of any present, Emolument, Office, or Title, of any kind whatever, from any King, Prince, or foreign State.

SECTION. 10. No State shall enter into any Treaty, Alliance, or Confederation; grant Letters of Marque and Reprisal; coin Money; emit Bills of Credit; make any Thing but gold and silver

*But see the sixteenth amendment.

Coin a Tender in Payment of Debts; pass any Bill of Attainder, ex post facto Law, or Law impairing the Obligation of Contracts, or grant any Title of Nobility.

No State shall, without the Consent of the Congress, lay any Imposts or Duties on Imports or Exports, except what may be absolutely necessary for executing its inspection Laws: and the net Produce of all Duties and Imposts, laid by any State on Imports or Exports, shall be for the Use of the Treasury of the United States; and all such Laws shall be subject to the Revision and Control of the Congress.

No State shall, without the Consent of Congress, lay any duty of Tonnage, keep Troops, or Ships of War in time of Peace, enter into any Agreement or Compact with another State, or with a foreign Power, or engage in War, unless actually invaded, or in such imminent Danger as will not admit of delay.

ARTICLE. II.

SECTION. 1. The executive Power shall be vested in a President of the United States of America. He shall hold his Office during the Term of four Years, and, together with the Vice President, chosen for the same Term, be elected, as follows.

Each State shall appoint, in such Manner as the Legislature thereof may direct, a Number of Electors, equal to the whole Number of Senators and Representatives to which the State may be entitled in the Congress: but no Senator or Representative, or Person holding an Office of Trust or Profit under the United States, shall be appointed an Elector.

[The Electors shall meet in their respective States, and vote by Ballot for two persons, of whom one at least shall not be an Inhabitant of the same State with themselves. And they shall make a List of all the Persons voted for, and of the Number of Votes for each; which List they shall sign and certify and transmit sealed to the Seat of the Government of the United States, directed to the President of the Senate. The President of the Senate shall, in the Presence of the Senate and House of Representatives, open all the Certificates, and the Votes shall then be counted. The Person having the greatest Number of Votes shall be the President, if such Number be a Majority of the whole Number of Electors appointed; and if there be more than one who have such Majority, and have an equal Number of Votes, then the House of Representatives shall immediately chuse by Ballot one of them for President; and if no Person have a Majority, then from the five highest on the List the said House shall in like Manner chuse the President. But in chusing the President, the Votes shall be taken by States, the Representation from each State having one Vote; a quorum for this Purpose shall consist of a Member or Members from two thirds of the States, and a Majority of all the States shall be necessary to a Choice. In every Case, after the Choice of the President, the Person having the greatest Number of Votes of the Electors shall be the Vice President. But if there should remain two or more who have equal Votes, the Senate shall chuse from them by Ballot the Vice President.]*

The Congress may determine the Time of chusing the Electors, and the Day on which they shall give their Votes; which Day shall be the same throughout the United States.

No person except a natural born Citizen, or a Citizen of the United States, at the time of the Adoption of this Constitution, shall be eligible to the Office of President; neither shall any Person be eligible to that Office who shall not have attained to the Age of thirty five Years, and been fourteen Years a Resident within the United States.

[In Case of the Removal of the President from Office, or of his Death, Resignation, or Inability to discharge the Powers and Duties of the said Office, the same shall devolve on the Vice President, and the Congress may by Law provide for the Case of Removal, Death, Resignation or Inability, both of the President and Vice President, declaring what Officer shall then act as President, and such Officer shall act accordingly, until the Disability be removed, or a President shall be elected.]**

The President shall, at stated Times, receive for his Services, a Compensation, which shall neither be increased nor diminished during the Period for which he shall have been elected, and he shall not receive within that Period any other Emolument from the United States, or any of them.

Before he enter on the Execution of his Office, he shall take the following Oath or Affirmation:—"I do solemnly swear (or affirm) that I will faithfully execute the Office of President of the United States, and will to the best of my Ability, preserve, protect and defend the Constitution of the United States."

*Superseded by the twelfth amendment.
**This clause was amended by the twentieth amendment, sections three and four, and has been affected by the twenty-fifth amendment.

SECTION. 2. The President shall be Commander in Chief of the Army and Navy of the United States, and of the Militia of the several States, when called into the actual Service of the United States; he may require the Opinion in writing, of the principal Officer in each of the executive Departments, upon any subject relating to the Duties of their respective Offices, and he shall have Power to Grant Reprieves and Pardons for Offenses against the United States, except in Cases of Impeachment.

He shall have Power, by and with the Advice and Consent of the Senate, to make Treaties, provided two thirds of the Senators present concur; and he shall nominate, and by and with the Advice and Consent of the Senate, shall appoint Ambassadors, other public Ministers and Consuls, Judges of the supreme Court, and all other Officers of the United States, whose Appointments are not herein otherwise provided for, and which shall be established by Law: but the Congress may by Law vest the Appointment of such inferior Officers, as they think proper, in the President alone, in the Courts of Law, or in the Heads of Departments.

The President shall have Power to fill up all Vacancies that may happen during the Recess of the Senate, by granting Commissions which shall expire at the End of their next Session.

SECTION. 3. He shall from time to time give to the Congress Information of the State of the Union, and recommend to their Consideration such Measures as he shall judge necessary and expedient; he may, on extraordinary Occasions, convene both Houses, or either of them, and in Case of Disagreement between them, with Respect to the Time of Adjournment, he may adjourn them to such Time as he shall think proper; he shall receive Ambassadors and other public Ministers; he shall take Care that the Laws be faithfully executed, and shall Commission all the Officers of the United States.

SECTION. 4. The President, Vice President and all civil Officers of the United States, shall be removed from Office on Impeachment for, and Conviction of, Treason, Bribery, or other high Crimes and Misdemeanors.

ARTICLE. III.

SECTION. I. The judicial Power of the United States, shall be vested in one supreme Court, and in such inferior Courts as the Congress may from time to time ordain and establish. The Judges, both of the supreme and inferior Courts, shall hold their

Offices during good Behaviour, and shall, at stated Times, receive for their Services, a Compensation, which shall not be diminished during their Continuance in Office.

SECTION. 2. The judicial Power shall extend to all Cases, in Law and Equity, arising under this Constitution, the Laws of the United States, and Treaties made, or which shall be made, under their Authority;—to all Cases affecting Ambassadors, other public Ministers and Consuls,—to all Cases of admiralty and maritime Jurisdiction;—to Controversies to which the United States shall be a Party;—to Controversies between two or more States;—between a State and Citizens of another State;—between Citizens of different States;—between Citizens of the same State claiming Lands under Grants of different States, and between a State, or the Citizens thereof, and foreign States, Citizens or Subjects.*

In all Cases affecting Ambassadors, other public Ministers and Consuls, and those in which a State shall be Party, the supreme Court shall have original Jurisdiction. In all the other Cases before mentioned, the supreme Court shall have appellate Jurisdiction, both as to Law and Fact, with such Exceptions, and under such Regulations as the Congress shall make.

The Trial of all Crimes, except in Cases of Impeachment, shall be by Jury; and such Trial shall be held in the State where the said Crimes shall have been committed; but when not committed within any State, the Trial shall be at such Place or Places as the Congress may by Law have directed.

SECTION. 3. Treason against the United States, shall consist only in levying War against them, or in adhering to their Enemies, giving them Aid and Comfort. No Person shall be convicted of Treason unless on the Testimony of two Witnesses to the same overt Act, or on Confession in open Court.

The Congress shall have Power to declare the Punishment of Treason, but no Attainder of Treason shall work Corruption of Blood, or Forfeiture except during the Life of the Person attainted.

ARTICLE. IV.

SECTION. I. Full Faith and Credit shall be given in each State to the public Acts, Records, and judicial Proceedings of every

---

*This clause has been affected by the eleventh amendment.

other State. And the Congress may by general Laws prescribe the Manner in which such Acts, Records and Proceedings shall be proved, and the Effect thereof.

SECTION. 2. The Citizens of each State shall be entitled to all Privileges and Immunities of Citizens in the several States.

A Person charged in any State with Treason, Felony, or other Crime, who shall flee from Justice, and be found in another State, shall on Demand of the executive Authority of the State from which he fled, be delivered up, to be removed to the State having Jurisdiction of the Crime.

[No Person held to Service or Labour in one State, under the Laws thereof, escaping into another, shall, in Consequence of any Law or Regulation therein, be discharged from such Service or Labour, but shall be delivered up on Claim of the Party to whom such Service or Labour may be due.]*

SECTION. 3. New States may be admitted by the Congress into this Union; but no new State shall be formed or erected within the Jurisdiction of any other State; nor any State be formed by the Junction of two or more States, or Parts of States, without the Consent of the Legislatures of the States concerned as well as of the Congress.

The Congress shall have Power to dispose of and make all needful Rules and Regulations respecting the Territory or other Property belonging to the United States; and nothing in this Constitution shall be so construed as to Prejudice any Claims of the United States, or of any particular State.

SECTION. 4. The United States shall guarantee to every State in this Union a Republican Form of Government, and shall protect each of them against Invasion; and on Application of the Legislature, or of the Executive (when the Legislature cannot be convened) against domestic Violence.

ARTICLE. V.

The Congress, whenever two thirds of both Houses shall deem it necessary, shall propose Amendments to this Constitution, or, on the Application of the Legislatures of two thirds of the several States, shall call a Convention for proposing Amendments, which, in either Case, shall be valid to all Intents and Purposes, as part of this Constitution, when ratified by the Legislatures of

*Superseded by the thirteenth amendment.

three fourths of the several States, or by Conventions in three fourths thereof, as the one or the other Mode of Ratification may be proposed by the Congress; Provided that no Amendment which may be made prior to the Year One thousand eight hundred and eight shall in any Manner affect the first and fourth Clauses in the Ninth Section of the first Article; and that no State, without its Consent, shall be deprived of its equal Suffrage in the Senate.

ARTICLE. VI.

All Debts contracted and Engagements entered into, before the Adoption of this Constitution, shall be as valid against the United States under this Constitution, as under the Confederation.

This Constitution, and the Laws of the United States which shall be made in Pursuance thereof; and all Treaties made, or which shall be made, under the Authority of the United States, shall be the supreme Law of the Land; and the Judges in every State shall be bound thereby, any Thing in the Constitution or Laws of any State to the Contrary notwithstanding.

The Senators and Representatives before mentioned, and the Members of the several State Legislatures, and all executive and judicial Officers, both of the United States and of the several States, shall be bound by Oath or Affirmation, to support this Constitution; but no religious Test shall ever be required as a Qualification to any Office or public Trust under the United States.

ARTICLE. VII.

The Ratification of the Conventions of nine States, shall be sufficient for the Establishment of this Constitution between the States so ratifying the Same.

Done in Convention by the Unanimous Consent of the States present the Seventeenth Day of September in the Year of our Lord one thousand seven hundred and Eighty seven and of the Independence of the United States of America the Twelfth. In Witness whereof We have hereunto subscribed our Names.

Go WASHINGTON
Presidt and deputy from Virginia

New Hampshire
JOHN LANGDON
NICHOLAS GILMAN

Massachusetts
NATHANIEL GORHAM
RUFUS KING

New Jersey
WIL: LIVINGSTON
DAVID BREARLEY
WM PATERSON
JONA: DAYTON

Virginia
JOHN BLAIR—
JAMES MADISON JR.

North Carolina
WM BLOUNT
HU WILLIAMSON
RICHD DOBBS SPAIGHT

South Carolina
J. RUTLEDGE
CHARLES PINCKNEY
CHARLES COTESWORTH PINCKNEY
PIERCE BUTLER

Georgia
WILLIAM FEW
ABR BALDWIN

Connecticut
WM SAML JOHNSON
ROGER SHERMAN

New York
ALEXANDER HAMILTON

Maryland
JAMES MCHENRY
DANL CARROL
DAN OF ST THOS JENIFER

Pennsylvania
B FRANKLIN
ROBT MORRIS
THOS FITZSIMONS
JAMES WILSON
THOMAS MIFFLIN
GEO. CLYMER
JARED INGERSOLL
GOUV MORRIS

Delaware
GEO: READ
JOHN DICKINSON
JACO: BROOM
GUNNING BEDFORD Jun
RICHARD BASSETT

Attest: WILLIAM JACKSON, *Secretary*

ARTICLES IN ADDITION TO, AND AMENDMENT OF, THE CONSTITUTION OF THE UNITED STATES OF AMERICA, PROPOSED BY CONGRESS, AND RATIFIED BY THE LEGISLATURES OF THE SEVERAL STATES, PURSUANT TO THE FIFTH ARTICLE OF THE ORIGINAL CONSTITUTION.*
(The first 10 Amendments were ratified December 15, 1791, and form what is known as the "Bill of Rights")

*Amendment XXI was not ratified by state legislatures, but by state conventions summoned by Congress.

AMENDMENT I.

Congress shall make no law respecting an establishment of religion, or prohibiting the free exercise thereof; or abridging the freedom of speech, or of the press; or the right of the people peaceably to assemble, and to petition the Government for a redress of grievances.

AMENDMENT II.

A well regulated Militia, being necessary to the security of a free State, the right of the people to keep and bear Arms, shall not be infringed.

AMENDMENT III.

No Soldier shall, in time of peace be quartered in any house, without the consent of the Owner, nor in time of war, but in a manner to be prescribed by law.

AMENDMENT IV.

The right of the people to be secure in their persons, houses, papers, and effects, against unreasonable searches and seizures, shall not be violated, and no Warrants shall issue, but upon probable cause, supported by Oath or affirmation, and particularly describing the place to be searched, and the persons or things to be seized.

AMENDMENT V.

No person shall be held to answer for a capital, or otherwise infamous crime, unless on a presentment or indictment of a Grand Jury, except in cases arising in the land or naval forces, or in the Militia, when in actual service in time of War or public danger; nor shall any person be subject for the same offence to be twice put in jeopardy of life or limb; nor shall be compelled in any criminal case to be a witness against himself, nor be deprived of life, liberty, or property, without due process of law; nor shall private property be taken for public use without just compensation.

AMENDMENT VI.

In all criminal prosecutions, the accused shall enjoy the right to a speedy and public trial, by an impartial jury of the State and district wherein the crime shall have been committed, which district shall have been previously ascertained by law, and to be informed of the nature and cause of the accusation; to be confronted with the witnesses against him; to have compulsory process for obtaining witnesses in his favor, and to have the Assistance of Counsel for his defence.

AMENDMENT VII.

In Suits at common law, where the value in controversy shall exceed twenty dollars, the right of trial by jury shall be preserved, and no fact tried by a jury, shall be otherwise re-examined in any Court of the United States, than according to the rules of the common law.

AMENDMENT VIII.

Excessive bail shall not be required, nor excessive fines imposed, nor cruel and unusual punishments inflicted.

AMENDMENT IX.

The enumeration in the Constitution of certain rights, shall not be construed to deny or disparage others retained by the people.

AMENDMENT X.

The powers not delegated to the United States by the Constitution, nor prohibited by it to the States, are reserved to the States respectively, or to the people.

AMENDMENT XI.

(Ratified February 7, 1795)

The Judicial power of the United States shall not be construed to extend to any suit in law or equity, commenced or prosecuted against one of the United States by Citizens of another State, or by Citizens or Subjects of any Foreign State.

AMENDMENT XII.

(Ratified June 15, 1804)

The Electors shall meet in their respective states and vote by ballot for President and Vice-President, one of whom, at least, shall not be an inhabitant of the same state with themselves; they shall name in their ballots the person voted for as President, and in distinct ballots the person voted for as Vice-President, and they shall make distinct lists of all persons voted for as President, and of all persons voted for as Vice-President, and of the number of votes for each, which lists they shall sign and certify, and transmit sealed to the seat of the government of the United States, directed to the President of the Senate—The President of the Senate shall, in presence of the Senate and House of Representatives, open all the certificates and the votes shall then be counted;—The person having the greatest number of votes for President, shall be the President, if such number be a majority of the whole number of Electors appointed; and if no person have such majority, then from the persons having the highest numbers not exceeding three on the list of those voted for as President, the House of Representatives shall choose immediately, by ballot, the President. But in choosing the President, the votes shall be taken by states, the representation from each state having one vote; a quorum for this purpose shall consist of a member or members from two-thirds of the states, and a majority of all the states shall be necessary to a choice. [And if the House of Representatives shall not choose a President whenever the right of choice shall devolve upon them, before the fourth day of March next following, then the Vice-President shall act as President, as in the case of the death or other constitutional disability of the President.—]* The person having the greatest number of votes as Vice-President, shall be the Vice-President, if such number be a majority of the whole number of Electors appointed, and if no person have a majority, then from the two highest numbers on the list, the Senate shall choose the Vice-President; a quorum for the purpose shall consist of two-thirds of the whole number of Senators, and a majority of the whole number shall be necessary to a choice. But no person constitutionally ineligible to the office of President shall be eligible to that of Vice-President of the United States.

*Superseded by section 3 of the twentieth amendment.

AMENDMENT XIII.

(Ratified December 6, 1865)

SECTION 1. Neither slavery nor involuntary servitude, except as a punishment for crime whereof the party shall have been duly convicted, shall exist within the United States, or any place subject to their jurisdiction.

SECTION 2. Congress shall have power to enforce this article by appropriate legislation.

AMENDMENT XIV.

(Ratified July 9, 1868)

SECTION 1. All persons born or naturalized in the United States, and subject to the jurisdiction thereof, are citizens of the United States and of the State wherein they reside. No State shall make or enforce any law which shall abridge the privileges or immunities of citizens of the United States; nor shall any State deprive any person of life, liberty, or property, without due process of law; nor deny to any person within its jurisdiction the equal protection of the laws.

SECTION 2. Representatives shall be apportioned among the several States according to their respective numbers, counting the whole number of persons in each State, excluding Indians not taxed. But when the right to vote at any election for the choice of electors for President and Vice President of the United States, Representatives in Congress, the Executive and Judicial officers of a State, or the members of the Legislature thereof, is denied to any of the male inhabitants of such State, being twenty-one years of age,* and citizens of the United States, or in any way abridged, except for participation in rebellion, or other crime, the basis of representation therein shall be reduced in the proportion which the number of such male citizens shall bear to the whole number of male citizens twenty-one years of age in such State.

SECTION 3. No person shall be a Senator or Representative in Congress, or elector of President and Vice President, or hold any office, civil or military, under the United States, or under any State, who, having previously taken an oath, as a member of Congress, or as an officer of the United States, or as a member of

---

*Superseded by section 1 of the twenty-sixth amendment.

any State legislature, or as an executive or judicial officer of any State, to support the Constitution of the United States, shall have engaged in insurrection or rebellion against the same, or given aid or comfort to the enemies thereof. But Congress may by a vote of two-thirds of each House, remove such disability.

SECTION 4. The validity of the public debt of the United States, authorized by law, including debts incurred for payment of pensions and bounties for services in suppressing insurrection or rebellion, shall not be questioned. But neither the United States nor any State shall assume or pay any debt or obligation incurred in aid of insurrection or rebellion against the United States, or any claim for the loss or emancipation of any slave; but all such debts, obligations and claims shall be held illegal and void.

SECTION 5. The Congress shall have power to enforce, by appropriate legislation, the provisions of this article.

AMENDMENT XV.

(Ratified February 3, 1870)

SECTION 1. The right of citizens of the United States to vote shall not be denied or abridged by the United States or by any State on account of race, color, or previous condition of servitude.

SECTION 2. The Congress shall have power to enforce this article by appropriate legislation.

AMENDMENT XVI.

(Ratified February 3, 1913)

The Congress shall have power to lay and collect taxes on incomes, from whatever source derived, without apportionment among the several States, and without regard to any census or enumeration.

AMENDMENT XVII.

(Ratified April 8, 1913)

The Senate of the United States shall be composed of two Senators from each State, elected by the people thereof, for six years; and each Senator shall have one vote. The electors in each State shall have the qualifications requisite for electors of the most numerous branch of the State legislatures.

When vacancies happen in the representation of any State in the Senate, the executive authority of such State shall issue writs of election to fill such vacancies: *Provided*, That the legislature of any State may empower the executive thereof to make temporary appointments until the people fill the vacancies by election as the legislature may direct.

This amendment shall not be so construed as to affect the election or term of any Senator chosen before it becomes valid as part of the Constitution.

AMENDMENT XVIII.

(Ratified January 16, 1919)

SECTION 1. After one year from the ratification of this article the manufacture, sale, or transportation of intoxicating liquors within, the importation thereof into, or the exportation thereof from the United States and all territory subject to the jurisdiction thereof for beverage purposes is hereby prohibited.

SECTION 2. The Congress and the several States shall have concurrent power to enforce this article by appropriate legislation.

SECTION 3. This article shall be inoperative unless it shall have been ratified as an amendment to the Constitution by the legislatures of the several States as provided in the Constitution, within seven years from the date of the submission hereof to the States by the Congress.*

AMENDMENT XIX.

(Ratified August 18, 1920)

The right of citizens of the United States to vote shall not be denied or abridged by the United States or by any State on account of sex.

Congress shall have power to enforce this article by appropriate legislation.

*Repealed by section 1 of the twenty-first amendment.

AMENDMENT XX.

(Ratified January 23, 1933)

SECTION 1. The terms of the President and Vice President shall end at noon on the twentieth day of January, and the terms of Senators and Representatives at noon on the third day of January, of the years in which such terms would have ended if this article had not been ratified; and the terms of their successors shall then begin.

SECTION 2. The Congress shall assemble at least once in every year, and such meeting shall begin at noon on the third day of January, unless they shall by law appoint a different day.

SECTION 3. If, at the time fixed for the beginning of the term of the President, the President elect shall have died, the Vice President shall become President. If a President shall not have been chosen before the time fixed for the beginning of his term, or if the President elect shall have failed to qualify, then the Vice President elect shall act as President until a President shall have qualified; and the Congress may by law provide for the case wherein neither a President elect nor a Vice President elect shall have qualified, declaring who shall then act as President, or the manner in which one who is to act shall be selected, and such person shall act accordingly until a President or Vice President shall have qualified.

SECTION 4. The Congress may by law provide for the case of the death of any of the persons from whom the House of Representatives may choose a President whenever the right of choice shall have devolved upon them, and for the case of the death of any of the persons from whom the Senate may choose a Vice President whenever the right of choice shall have devolved upon them.

SECTION 5. Sections 1 and 2 shall take effect on the 15th day of October following the ratification of this article.

SECTION 6. This article shall be inoperative unless it shall have been ratified as an amendment to the Constitution by the legislatures of three-fourths of the several States within seven years from the date of its submission.

AMENDMENT XXI.

(Ratified December 5, 1933)

SECTION I. The eighteenth article of amendment to the Constitution of the United States is hereby repealed.

SECTION 2. The transportation or importation into any State, territory, or possession of the United States for delivery or use therein of intoxicating liquors, in violation of the laws thereof, is hereby prohibited.

SECTION 3. This article shall be inoperative unless it shall have been ratified as an amendment to the Constitution by conventions in the several States, as provided in the Constitution, within seven years from the date of the submission hereof to the States by the Congress.

AMENDMENT XXII.

(Ratified February 27, 1951)

SECTION I. No person shall be elected to the office of the President more than twice, and no person who has held the office of President, or acted as President, for more than two years of a term to which some other person was elected President shall be elected to the office of the President more than once. But this Article shall not apply to any person holding the office of President when this article was proposed by the Congress, and shall not prevent any person who may be holding the office of President, or acting as President, during the term within which this Article becomes operative from holding the office of President or acting as President during the remainder of such term.

SECTION 2. This article shall be inoperative unless it shall have been ratified as an amendment to the Constitution by the legislatures of three-fourths of the several States within seven years from the date of its submission to the States by the Congress.

AMENDMENT XXIII.

(Ratified March 29, 1961)

SECTION I. The District constituting the seat of Government of the United States shall appoint in such manner as the Congress may direct:

A number of electors of President and Vice President equal to the whole number of Senators and Representatives in Congress to which the District would be entitled if it were a State, but in no event more than the least populous State; they shall be in addition to those appointed by the States, but they shall be considered, for the purposes of the election of President and Vice President, to be electors appointed by a State; and they shall meet in the District and perform such duties as provided by the twelfth article of amendment.

SECTION 2. The Congress shall have power to enforce this article by appropriate legislation.

AMENDMENT XXIV.

(Ratified January 23, 1964)

SECTION I. The right of citizens in the United States to vote in any primary or other election for President or Vice President, for electors for President or Vice President, or for Senator or Representative in Congress, shall not be denied or abridged by the United States or any State by reason of failure to pay any poll tax or other tax.

SECTION 2. The Congress shall have power to enforce this article by appropriate legislation.

AMENDMENT XXV.

(Ratified February 10, 1967)

SECTION 1. In case of the removal of the President from office or of his death or resignation, the Vice President shall become President.

SECTION 2. Whenever there is a vacancy in the office of the Vice President, the President shall nominate a Vice President who shall take office upon confirmation by a majority vote of both Houses of Congress.

SECTION 3. Whenever the President transmits to the President pro tempore of the Senate and the Speaker of the House of Representatives his written declaration that he is unable to discharge the powers and duties of his office, and until he transmits to them a written declaration to the contrary, such powers and duties shall be discharged by the Vice President as Acting President.

SECTION 4. Whenever the Vice President and a majority of either the principal officers of the executive departments or of such other body as Congress may by law provide, transmit to the President pro tempore of the Senate and the Speaker of the House of Representatives their written declaration that the President is unable to discharge the powers and duties of his office, the Vice President shall immediately assume the powers and duties of the office as Acting President.

Thereafter, when the President transmits to the President pro tempore of the Senate and the Speaker of the House of Representatives his written declaration that no inability exists, he shall resume the powers and duties of his office unless the Vice President and a majority of either the principal officers of the executive department or of such other body as Congress may by law provide, transmit within four days to the President pro tempore of the Senate and the Speaker of the House of Representatives their written declaration that the President is unable to discharge the powers and duties of his office. Thereupon Congress shall decide the issue, assembling within forty-eight hours for that purpose if not in session. If the Congress, within twenty-one days after receipt of the latter written declaration, or, if Congress is not in session, within twenty-one days after Congress is required to assemble, determines by two-thirds vote of both Houses that the President is unable to discharge the powers and duties of his office, the Vice President shall continue to discharge the same as Acting President; otherwise, the President shall resume the powers and duties of his office.

AMENDMENT XXVI.

(Ratified July 1, 1971)

SECTION I. The right of citizens of the United States, who are eighteen years of age or older, to vote shall not be denied or abridged by the United States or by any State on account of age.

SECTION 2. The Congress shall have power to enforce this article by appropriate legislation.

AMENDMENT XXVII.

(Ratified May 7, 1992)

No law, varying the compensation for the services of the Senators and Representatives, shall take effect, until an election of Representatives shall have intervened.

THE EMANCIPATION PROCLAMATION

JANUARY 1, 1863

Whereas, on the twenty-second day of September, in the year of our Lord one thousand eight hundred and sixty-two, a proclamation was issued by the President of the United States, containing, among other things, the following, to wit:

"That on the first day of January, in the year of our Lord one thousand eight hundred and sixty-three, all persons held as slaves within any state or designated part of a state, the people whereof shall then be in rebellion against the United States, shall be then, thenceforward, and forever, free; and the Executive Government of the United States, including the military and naval authority thereof, will recognize and maintain the freedom of such persons and will do no act or acts to repress such persons, or any of them, in any efforts they may make for their actual freedom.

"That the Executive will, on the first day of January aforesaid, by proclamation, designate the states and parts of states, if any, in which the people thereof, respectively, shall then be in rebellion against the United States, and the fact that any state, or the people thereof, shall on that day be in good faith represented in the Congress of the United States, by members chosen thereto at elections wherein a majority of the qualified voters of such states shall have participated shall, in the absence of strong countervailing testimony, be deemed conclusive evidence that such state, and the people thereof, are not then in rebellion against the United States."

Now, therefore, I, Abraham Lincoln, President of the United States, by virtue of the power in me vested as Commander-in-Chief of the Army and Navy of the United States, in time of actual armed rebellion against the authority and government of the United States, and as a fit and necessary war measure for suppressing said rebellion, do, on this first day of January, in the year of our Lord one thousand eight hundred and sixty-three, and in accordance with my purpose so to do, publicly proclaimed for the full period of one hundred days from the first day above mentioned, order and designate as the states and parts of states wherein the people thereof, respectively, are this day in rebellion against the United States, the following to wit:

Arkansas, Texas, Louisiana (except the parishes of St. Bernard, Plaquemines, Jefferson, St. Johns, St. Charles, St. James, Ascension, Assumption, Terrebonne, Lafourche, St. Mary, St. Martin, and Orleans, including the city of New Orleans), Mississippi, Alabama, Florida, Georgia, South Carolina, North Carolina, and Virginia (except the forty-eight counties designated as West Virginia, and also the counties of Berkeley, Accomac, Northampton, Elizabeth City, York, Princess Anne, and Norfolk, including the cities of Norfolk and Portsmouth) and which excepted parts are for the present left precisely as if this proclamation were not issued.

And by virtue of the power and for the purpose aforesaid, I do order and declare that all persons held as slaves within said designated states and parts of states are, and henceforward shall be, free; and that the Executive Government of the United States, including the military and Naval authorities thereof, will recognize and maintain the freedom of said persons.

And I hereby enjoin upon the people so declared to be free to abstain from all violence, unless in necessary self-defense; and I recommend to them that, all cases when allowed, they labor faithfully for reasonable wages.

And I further declare and make known that such persons of suitable condition will be received into the armed service of the United States to garrison forts, positions, stations, and other places, and to man vessels of all sorts in said service.

And upon this act, sincerely believed to be an act of justice, warranted by the Constitution upon military necessity, I invoke the considerate judgment of mankind and the gracious favor of Almighty God.

In witness whereof, I have hereunto set my hand and caused the seal of the United States to be affixed.

Done at the city of Washington this first day of January, in the year of our Lord one thousand eight hundred and sixty-three, and of the Independence of the United States of America the eighty-seventh.

Abraham Lincoln

THE PRESIDENTS
of the United States of America

George Washington	1789–1797
John Adams	1797–1801
Thomas Jefferson	1801–1809
James Madison	1809–1817
James Monroe	1817–1825
John Quincy Adams	1825–1829
Andrew Jackson	1829–1837
Martin Van Buren	1837–1841
William Henry Harrison	1841
John Tyler	1841–1845
James K. Polk	1845–1849
Zachary Taylor	1849–1850
Millard Fillmore	1850–1853
Franklin Pierce	1853–1857
James Buchanan	1857–1861
Abraham Lincoln	1861–1865
Andrew Johnson	1865–1869
Ulysses S. Grant	1869–1877
Rutherford B. Hayes	1877–1881
James A. Garfield	1881
Chester A. Arthur	1881–1885
Grover Cleveland	1885–1889; 1893–1897
Benjamin Harrison	1889–1893
William McKinley	1897–1901
Theodore Roosevelt	1901–1909
William H. Taft	1909–1913
Woodrow Wilson	1913–1921
Warren G. Harding	1921–1923
Calvin Coolidge	1923–1929
Herbert Hoover	1929–1933
Franklin D. Roosevelt	1933–1945
Harry S. Truman	1945–1953
Dwight D. Eisenhower	1953–1961
John F. Kennedy	1961–1963
Lyndon B. Johnson	1963–1969
Richard M. Nixon	1969–1974
Gerald R. Ford	1974–1977
Jimmy Carter	1977–1981
Ronald Reagan	1981–1989
George Bush	1989–1993
William J. Clinton	1993–2001
George W. Bush	2001–

Milestones in American History

Jamestown, Virginia, founded by the British	1607
The Pilgrims establish Plymouth colony	1620
The Mayflower Compact	1626
Dominion of New England established	May 25, 1686
The Boston Massacre	March 5, 1770
Battle of Bunker Hill (Revolutionary War begins)	June 17, 1775
Declaration of Independence	July 4, 1776
Treaty of Paris, peace with Britain	1783
Constitution is approved	September 17, 1787
The Bill of Rights becomes part of Constitution	December 15, 1791
Louisiana Territory sold to the U.S. by France	1803
The Lewis & Clark Expedition arrives in Oregon	1805
War of 1812	1812–1814
Florida ceded to the United States by Spain	1819
The Nat Turner Revolt	1831
The Mexican War	1846–1847
Gold is discovered in California	1848
Civil War	1861–1865
Emancipation Proclamation	January 1, 1863
Alaska sold to the U.S. by Czar Alexander II	1867
Wounded Knee Massacre	January 1, 1891
Spanish–American War	1898
Panama Canal opens	1914
U.S. entry into World War I	1917
Armistice in Europe	1918
Stock Market Crash	October 29, 1929
U.S. entry into World War II	December 8, 1941
Victory over Germany	May 5, 1945
Victory over Japan	August 14, 1945
Alaska and Hawaii enter the Union	1959
Korean War	1950–1953
Cuban Missile Crisis	1962
Vietnam War	1965–1973
Martin Luther King is assassinated	April 4, 1968
U.S. astronauts land on the moon	July 16, 1969
Gulf War	August 2, 1990–February 28, 1991
Terrorist Attack on the United States	**September 11, 2001**

Notes

Patrick Henry, portrait by Thomas Sully, courtesy of Colonial Williamsburg Foundation.

The speech from which these passages are excerpted was delivered before the Virginia Convention, which was then debating "The Resolution to Put the Commonwealth into a State of Defence." As printed in Louie R. Heller, ed., *Early American Orators, 1760–1824* (Freeport, NY, 1902), pp. 51–54. Patrick Henry's fiery oratory helped rouse the nation to the cause of the Revolution.

John Adams, portrait by George Healey, in the collection of the Corcoran Gallery of Art. Museum purchase, Gallery Fund, 1879.

Letter to his wife, Abigail Adams, printed in *Letters of John Adams to His Wife*, Vol. I, pp. 109–111. John Adams's correspondence with his wife, Abigail, is a most informative source on the American Revolution. Adams is noted for having developed the first systematic political theory of the American system of government. He served as the country's second president.

Thomas McKean, portrait attributed to Charles Willson Peale, courtesy of the National Portrait Gallery, Smithsonian Institution.

Letter cited in John M. Coleman, *Thomas McKean, Forgotten Leader of the Revolution* (American Faculty Press: Rockaway, NJ, 1975), p. 160.

One of the leading politicians who took part in the American Revolution, Thomas McKean was a native of Pennsylvania, serving as that state's Chief Justice and Governor.

The State House in Philadelphia, northwest view, taken in 1778. Engraving by J. Trunchard after C. W. Peale, from the *Columbian Magazine*, 1787, Courtesy of Independence National Historical Park Collection.

Samuel Adams, portrait by Jonathan Singleton Copley, courtesy of the Museum of Fine Arts, Boston.
Samuel Adams, who has become known as "The Father of the American Revolution," delivered this speech at Philadelphia not long after the signing of the Declaration of Independence. It is the only speech of his that has been preserved in writing. From Louie R. Heller, ed., *Early American Orators, 1760–1824* (Freeport, NY, 1902), pp. 74–84.

Benjamin Franklin, portrait by Joseph Wright, in the collection of the Corcoran Gallery of Art. Museum purchase.
1. Letter to Charles de Weissenstein, July 1, 1778, reprinted in Benjamin Franklin, *Writings*, edited by J. A. Leo Lemay, (The Library of America: New York, 1987), p. 1001.
2. Letter to Jonathan Shipley, February 24, 1786, reprinted in *ibid.*, p. 1161.
3. "Speech in the Convention at the Conclusion of its Deliberations," Sept. 17, 1787, in *ibid.*, p. 1140.
Franklin, who was primarily a scientist, and only reluctantly a politician, contributed to the victory of the Revolutionary forces by securing the alliance of France. He decisively affected the debate at the Constitutional Convention of 1787.

The Constitutional Convention, *The Signing of the U.S. Constitution*, by Howard Chandler Christy, architect of the Capitol, U.S. House of Representatives.

George Mason, portrait attributed to John Toole, courtesy of Virginia State Library and Archives.

George Mason of Virginia played a major role in forming the Constitution and was instrumental in getting the first ten amendments approved as the Bill of Rights. He refused to sign the Constitution in 1787 when it did not yet include the Bill.

Speeches cited in Helen Hill Miller, *George Mason: Gentleman Revolutionary* (The University of North Carolina Press: Chapel Hill, 1975), pp. 282, 294.

Alexander Hamilton, portrait courtesy of the Library of Congress.
1. *The Federalist*, No. 1. The First of the Federalist papers, in which Hamilton, writing under the pen name "Publius," sets the theme for the discussion.
2. "On the Federal Constitution," speech given on June 20, 1788, during a resumption of the Constitutional debate. As printed in Louie R. Heller, *op. cit.*, p. 88.

Alexander Hamilton is often considered the leading political theorist of the American Revolution, and is best known for his contribution to the cause of the union and the adoption of the Constitution by the thirteen states.

John Jay, portrait by Cornelius Tiebout, courtesy of the National Portrait Gallery, Smithsonian Institution.
1. *The Federalist*, No. 2, writing under the same pseudonym "Publius," commends the advantages of union to the American people.
2. John Jay wrote this opinion in his capacity of Chief Justice of the Supreme Court in the case of *Chisholm v. Georgia*, 2 Dall. 419 (1793), reprinted in *The Justices of the United States Supreme Court 1779–1978*, Vol. I (Chelsea House Publ.: New York, London, 1980), p. 24.

John Jay was by profession a lawyer, and he became the first Chief Justice of the United States.

Thomas Paine, portrait by George Romney, 1792, courtesy of the Library of Congress.

The Rights of Man, 1790. A cosmopolitan agitator and revolutionary, Thomas Paine came to America in 1774, just before the outbreak of the Revolutionary War, at the urging of Benjamin Franklin, because, as he said, it was "the only spot in the world where the principles of political reformation could begin." His political tracts, and *The Rights of Man* in particular, had enormous influence around the world.

George Washington, portrait by Charles Willson Peale, courtesy of The Pennsylvania Academy of the Fine Arts, Philadelphia. Bequest of Mrs. Sarah Harrison (the Joseph Harrison, Jr. collection).

"Letter to James Madison," May 20, 1792, reproduced in Saul K. Padover, *The Washington Papers* (Grosset & Dunlap: New York, 1967), p. 382.

George Washington's decisive political leadership and brilliant military tactics secured the success of the revolution. As the country's first president he firmly established the foundations of republican government.

James Madison, portrait courtesy of White House Historical Association.

1. *In Answer to "Pacificus,"* April 22, 1793. Reproduced in *The Complete Madison: His Basic Writings,* edited by Saul K. Padover (Harper & Bro., New York, 1953), p. 48.

2. *National Gazette,* February 20, 1792 in *ibid.,* p. 345.
   James Madison, who became the fourth president of the United States, is known as "the father of the Constitution" for his leading role at the 1787 Constitutional

Convention. He produced the first ten amendments to the Constitution, known as the "Bill of Rights."

Thomas Jefferson, portrait courtesy of White House Historical Association.
Letter to William Green Mumford, written at Monticello, June 18, 1799, reproduced in Adrienne Koch, ed., *Jefferson* (Prentice Hall: Englewood Cliffs, NJ, 1971). Thomas Jefferson, author of the Declaration of Independence, was the great philosopher-statesman of the American republic. He was a man of the Enlightenment, a scientist, an architect, and a political theorist of the first degree.

John Marshall, portrait by James Reid Lambdin, after the 1831 oil by Henry Inman. Courtesy of the National Portrait Gallery, Smithsonian Institution.
Opinion in the case of *Marbury v. Madison*, cited in John E. Oster, *The Political and Economic Doctrines of John Marshall* (Burt Franklin: New York, 1914.)
Chief Justice John Marshall is often regarded as one of the most statesmanlike figures in American judicial history. His decisions laid the foundations for the Supreme Court's role in the defense of the Constitution.

Henry Clay, courtesy of the Library of Congress.
Senator and Secretary of State, Clay played a major role in the efforts to keep the Union on an even keel through some of the most tumultuous years in its history.
Speeches cited in Glyndon G. van Deusen, *The Life of Henry Clay* (Little, Brown and Co.: Boston, 1937).

James Monroe, portrait by Rembrandt Peale, painted from life in 1824, in the collection of the James Monroe

Museum, Fredricksburg, Virginia.

James Monroe, *The People, The Sovereigns* (James River Press: Cumberland, Virginia, 1987), pp. 1–2.

Monroe, best remembered for the Monroe Doctrine that made the Western Hemisphere off limits to European colonization, was also an important political thinker. The book from which this passage is taken reflects a lifetime of experience and study (including a visit to revolutionary France and the Presidency).

Alexis de Tocqueville, sketch by Th. Chassériau, 1844.

1. *Democracy in America,* 1835, I. 57
2. *Ibid.,* I.172

This book, which has become a classic of political literature, was the product of de Tocqueville's extensive travels in America as member of a French government commission. In it, he attempted to draw lessons from the American experiment in self-government for Europe, then under the sway of absolute monarchies. De Tocqueville was able to put his findings into practice during the Revolution of 1848 and during his brief tenure as French foreign minister in 1849.

Andrew Jackson, portrait by Thomas Sully, courtesy of the National Gallery of Art, Andrew W. Mellon Collection.

Jackson, a populist and advocate of increased popular association in government, brought about an essential renewal of the American political system. He attacked monopolies and citadels of privilege. Later generations would use the expression "Jacksonian democracy" to describe his brand of broadly democratic social reformation. J.D. Richardson, ed., *Memoirs and Papers of the Presidents* (Washington, D.C., 1898) Vol. II, pp. 576ff.

John Quincy Adams, portrait by George Healey, in the collection of the Corcoran Gallery of Art. Museum purchase.

Adams's diaries provide revealing glimpses into the personality of this far-sighted foe of slavery. Charles Francis Adams, ed., *Memoirs of John Quincy Adams* (Boston, 1874–77), V, 11–12.

Albert Gallatin, portrait courtesy of the Independence National Historical Park Collection.

Albert Gallatin, *Peace with Mexico*, (Bartlett & Welford: New York, 1847) pp. 25ff.

A Swiss by birth, an American by choice, Albert Gallatin became a respected statesman in the service of the Jefferson and Madison administrations. After the War of 1812 broke out, he tirelessly pursued a peaceful settlement until his efforts were rewarded. His eloquent appeal for peace with Mexico was the final effort of a long and distinguished career dedicated to his country and to peace.

Henry David Thoreau, daguerreotype by Benjamin D. Maxham, 1856, courtesy of the National Portrait Gallery, Smithsonian Institution.

On the Duty of Civil Disobedience, The Aesthetic Papers, ed. by Elizabeth Peabody, 1849.

Thoreau's one-man experiment in individual freedom at Walden Pond inexorably led to conflict with authority. Events were brought to a head in 1846 with the outbreak of the Mexican War, which Thoreau saw as an attempt to extend slavery. When a poll-tax in support of war was enacted, Thoreau refused to pay it, and was briefly imprisoned. This experience gave rise to his bitter but powerful manifesto, which has become a rallying cry for non-violent resistance movements worldwide.

Daniel Webster, photograph courtesy of the Library of Congress.

Speech in Congress on March 7, 1850. From the *Congressional Globe Appendix*, 31 Cong., 1 Sess., pp. 269–276. Webster was one of the most impressive statesmen and orators of his time; but his efforts at preserving the Union despite the ever widening fault lines between North and South eventually met with failure.

James Buchanan, photograph made c. 1859 after c. 1856 daguerreotype by Charles and Henry Meade, courtesy of the National Portrait Gallery, Smithsonian Institution.

"Annual message to Congress," December 3, 1860. From James D. Richardson, ed., *A Compilation of the Messages and Papers of the Presidents, 1789–1897* (Washington, 1896–99), Vol. V, 626–639.

In Buchanan's time the cleavage between North and South assumed a scale such as to doom to failure his desperate efforts at preserving the Union.

Walt Whitman, photograph by Frederick Gutekunst, 1880, courtesy of the National Portrait Gallery, Smithsonian Institution.

Edward F. Grier, ed., *The Eighteenth Presidency!* (University of Kansas Press: Lawrence, Kansas, 1956), pp. 42–44. Walt Whitman wrote *The Eighteenth Presidency!* in the face of the approaching national tragedy. His premonition of the coming upheaval is couched in the poetic diction characteristic of his writing, but it contains the view that a war might, as a last resort, be the only way of resolving the crisis, and that a new sort of leadership was needed to bring the nation safely through the storm whose threatening clouds were already all too visible on the horizon.

Abraham Lincoln, photograph courtesy of the Library of Congress.

"Address at the Dedication of the Gettysburg National Cemetery," November 19, 1863, reprinted in *Abraham Lincoln, Letters and Addresses* (The Sundial Classics Co.: New York, 1908), pp. 289–290.

Lincoln led the nation through the most difficult crisis in its history, and in his two terms as president won a place in history second to none, equal to that of George Washington. In his Gettysburg address Lincoln eloquently summed up the issue facing the nation. He proved equal to the task, preserved the Union, abolished slavery, and began the arduous task of reconstruction. He was felled by an assassin's bullet on April 14, 1865.

Ulysses S. Grant, photograph by Federick Gutekunst, c. 1864, courtesy of the National Portrait Gallery, Smithsonian Institution.

Grant, the general who led the Federal Armies to victory in the Civil War and went on to become president, wrote his famous memoirs in the last year of his life. Mark Twain called this autobiography "the best of any general's since Caesar."

Ralph Waldo Emerson, photograph by Gerard A. Klucken, courtesy of the National Portrait Gallery, Smithsonian Institution.

1. "The Emancipation Proclamation, An Address Delivered in Boston in September, 1862," reprinted in Emerson, *Works* (Houghton Mifflin Co.: New York & Boston, 1883), Vol. 11, pp. 296ff.
2. "The Young American," *Dial*, IV (April, 1944), 484–507. The essay was delivered as a lecture before the Mercantile Library Association of Boston on

February 7, 1844.
Emerson was one of the most influential American writers of all time. His essays and lectures helped strengthen the forces opposed to slavery.

David Davis, photograph courtesy of Illinois State Historical Library, David Davis Family Papers, reproduced in Robert Shnayerson, *The Illustrated History of The Supreme Court of the United States* (Harry N. Abrams Inc.,: New York, 1986).
Opinion in the case "Ex Parte Milligan," in which a civilian appealed a death sentence passed on him by a military tribunal, following the suspension by President Lincoln on October 15, 1863, of the writ of habeas corpus in cases of persons arrested for military offences. Saul K. Padover, *The Living U.S. Constitution* (Praeger: New York, 1953).

Susan B. Anthony, photograph courtesy University of Rochester Library. Speech reproduced in Ellen Carol DuBois, ed., *Elizabeth Cady Stanton, Susan B. Anthony: Correspondence, Writings, Speeches* (Schocken Books: New York, 1981), pp. 153–154. Anthony developed her "Constitutional argument" following her arrest in November 1872 in Rochester for "illegal voting."

Frederick Douglass, photograph courtesy of S. B. Lieb Photo Co., York, Pennsylvania.
Speech at Commemorative meeting on 23rd anniversary of Emancipation Proclamation in Washington., D.C., April 1885. Reproduced in *The Mind and Heart of Frederick Douglass*, adapted by Barbara Ritchie (New York, 1968), pp. 186–187. Douglass, born a slave, rose to a position of great moral influence in nineteenth-century America. His autobiography, pub-

lished in 1845, strengthened the abolitionist cause. A confidant of Abraham Lincoln, Douglass remained a potent political force in the era of Reconstruction.

Theodore Roosevelt, photograph courtesy of the Library of Congress.
1. Hermann Hagedorn, *The Theodore Roosevelt Treasury* (G. P. Putnam's Sons: New York, 1953), pp. 306ff.
2. *Ibid.,* pp. 168–169.
   Theodore Roosevelt's presidency was characterized by rising prosperity at home and an active foreign policy, distinguished by such ventures as the building of the Panama Canal.

Woodrow Wilson, photograph courtesy of the Library of Congress.
   Woodrow Wilson's decision to engage the United States in the Great War against the Central Powers marked a turning point in that war, and secured for the United States a major role in constructing the postwar order in Europe.

Louis Brandeis, photograph courtesy of the Library of Congress.
   Opinion in the case of *Whitney v. California,* delivered in his capacity as Justice of the Supreme Court, 274 U.S 357. 375–377 (1927), reproduced in *The Justices of the United States Supreme Court 1779-1978,* vol. 3 (Chelsea House: New York and London, 1980), p. 2055.

Franklin Delano Roosevelt, photograph courtesy of the Library of Congress.
1. Address, May 26, 1940, reproduced in Donald Porter Geddes, ed., *Franklin Delano Roosevelt, A Memorial* (Pocket Books: New York, 1945), p. 174.

2. Message to Congress, January 1, 1939, *ibid.*, p. 173.
3. Third Inaugural Address, January 20, 1941, in *ibid.*, pp. 175–176.

   The long presidency of "FDR," as he was affectionately known to the American people, was a time of great social dislocations. FDR came into office at a time of economic catastrophe, and led his nation to a new confidence in its future, and to victory in the war against the Axis powers.

Harry S. Truman, photograph courtesy of the Library of Congress.

"Report on the Berlin Conference," radio address reprinted in Cyril Clemens ed., *Truman Speaks* (Webster Groves, Missouri, 1946), p. 70.

Truman, the straight-talking populist from Missouri, enjoyed the affection of the American people for his exemplary honesty and candor. He led the nation to victory over Germany and Japan, and laid the foundation of the postwar security system. He extended assistance to Western Europe and Japan that enabled them to rebuild their shattered economies and join America in the defense of the free world.

Walter Lippmann, photograph by Vytas Varaitas, courtesy of *Newsweek*.

U.S. War Aims (Little, Brown and Co.: Boston, 1945), pp. 208–210.

The century's most respected political commentator, Lippmann had a unique gift for formulating America's meaning and mission.

Henry Steele Commager, photograph by Gabriel A. Cooney, courtesy of Amherst College.

"Who Is Loyal to America?" *Harper's Magazine* (October, 1947), CXCV, 193–199.

Commager's article drew the line against the intellectual foundations of McCarthyism at the very outset. His arguments at last prevailed, but several years were to pass before this sad chapter in American history was definitively closed.

John F. Kennedy, photograph by David Lee Iwerks, courtesy of the National Portrait Gallery, Smithsonian Institution.

First Inaugural Address

Kennedy's short tenure in the Presidency was marked by an effort to revive the ideals of the American Revolution, while fostering democracy around the globe. His assassination on November 22, 1963, shocked the nation as few events have before or since.

Martin Luther King, Jr, photograph courtesy of the Library of Congress.

Speech at Lincoln Memorial, August 28, 1963, as printed in *SCLC Newsletter*, I (Sept., 1963), 5, 8.

Dr. Martin Luther King, America's greatest civil rights leader, has become the pre-eminent symbol of this country's commitment to the principles of its founders. His speech at the Lincoln Memorial, at the conclusion of the massive March on Washington, has become a classic of American oratory. It contains an eloquent summation of these principles as well as a challenge to the American people to aspire to them and abide by them. He was assassinated in Memphis on April 4, 1968.

Madeleine K. Albright, photograph courtesy of U.S. State Department.

"Sustaining Democracy in the Twenty-First Century,"

The Rostor Lecture Series, School of Advanced International Studies, Johns Hopkins University, Washington, DC, January 18, 2000 as released by the Office of the Spokesman, U.S. Department of State. Madeleine Albright, a native of Czechoslovakia, served as U.S. Secretary of State, the first woman to hold this post, from 1996 to 2001. Prior to her appointment, she served as the United States Permanent Representative to the United Nations and as a member of President Clinton's cabinet and National Security Council.